Swiss Country Inns
& Chalets

OTHER BOOKS IN KAREN BROWN'S COUNTRY INN SERIES

FRENCH COUNTRY INNS & CHATEAU HOTELS

ENGLISH, WELSH & SCOTTISH COUNTRY INNS

ITALIAN COUNTRY INNS & VILLAS

Scheduled for 1985:

Spanish Country Inns & Paradors

German Country Inns & Castle Hotels

Austrian Country Inns & Castle Hotels

Swiss Country Inns & Chalets

KAREN BROWN **and** **CLARE BROWN**

Illustrated by BARBARA TAPP

TRAVEL PRESS   San Mateo, California

Illustrations: BARBARA TAPP
Cover Design & Painting: BARBARA TAPP
Maps: BONNIE ROSSI

Editors: KAREN BROWN, CLARE BROWN, JUNE BROWN

This book is written as a publication for:

Town and Country Travel Service
16 East Third Avenue, San Mateo, California 94401

International Standard Book Number: 0-930328-11-6
Library of Contress Catalog Card Number: 84-052123
Printed in the United States of America

Distributed by

THE SCRIBNER BOOK COMPANIES, INC.

Travel Press   San Mateo, California

In Memory Of

MICHAEL

You will always be in our hearts

Foreword

It was over a spring weekend that the concept of my first travel guide, FRENCH COUNTRY INNS AND CHATEAU HOTELS, evolved. I was eager to return to Europe to study French, and my mother, who owns a travel agency, suggested that I attempt to finance my trip by researching a much needed guide to atmospheric inns and castle hotels. A guide that would also outline countryside itineraries. The idea developed and has proved marketable. FRENCH COUNTRY INNS AND CHATEAU HOTELS, first published in 1977, is now revised and in its second printing, and ENGLISH, WELSH AND SCOTTISH COUNTRY INNS AND CASTLE HOTELS appeared on the market in 1979.

While writing my previous books my family's constant encouragement lightened my task. This time, I am happy to say, they became involved in the actual research, travel, writing and production. It had been my intention to expand upon the "inn" series as quickly as possible, but this past year I couldn't seem to schedule in the months necessary to complete the required research. When my parents, Clare and Bill Brown, offered to revise their vacation plans, make Switzerland their travel destination and plan their route in order to investigate hotels, I was thrilled. I was confident that my mother, a natural in her role as travel agent (whom I remember as a child, dragging us, while on family vacations, through any and every promising hotel we passed) would love every moment. However travel, with research as its main objective, can be tiresome, and I was worried that the enthusiasm of my father, whose role was to be that of navigator, photographer and companion, would eventually wane. To my surprise, he became very involved in the project taking pictures, compiling historical, geographic and cultural notes and enjoyed the entire trip. The data they acquired completed the gaps in my initial research; blended beautifully with my earlier experiences and wonderful introduction to Switzerland when I lived there some years ago; and enabled us to ready the book for publication. Following the physical research, the hours at the computer, writing descriptions, outlining travel routes, sorting ideas and selecting words, were not tedious, but rather, quite enjoyable with Mom at my side!

SWISS COUNTRY INNS & CHALETS most definitely reflects and profits from a group involvement, the creative input of many, and a shared enthusiasm for an incredibly beautiful country! Looking back, hours were not only spent completing the project but securing what I hope will be some lifelong friendships. Lyle, a close friend visiting from Australia, introduced us to computers, incorporating word processing for the first time into our publishing framework. His contributions proved invaluable, dedicating long hours to evaluate and then install the best system. We, as novices, also unmercifully tested his patience, by asking endless questions and provoking terminal complications that not even the most versed computer expert would have anticipated!

Another Australian, darling Barbara, was also very involved in the production of this guide. Impressed by her artistic ability, I felt very fortunate that she agreed to do the hotel illustrations, but never imagined the extent that her influence would have on the book. Extremely dedicated, she has not only supplied an outstanding collection of hotel sketches, but also a constant stream of creative ideas and an infectious enthusiasm for the project. Barbara shares a love for Switzerland having been based there for over a year with her husband. They have two absolutely adorable boys, and although, I know they consider Australia home, I selfishly hope that they will remain here for many years to come. Barbara's friendship is one to value and cherish.

If SWISS COUNTRY INNS & CHALETS reflects only a sampling of the love, laughter and fun that went into it, I am confident that it will enhance, if not prove to be the best guide in the series. I have never enjoyed a publishing endeavor more and have only my family and friends to thank for their involvement and contributions.

Thank you,
Karen

Contents

HOTEL DESCRIPTIONS

SUPPLEMENTAL HOTEL DESCRIPTIONS

INDEX

Introduction

SWITZERLAND IS A COUNTRY of unchallengeable beauty, lofty peaks that dazzle the skies, lush alpine pastures that stretch between magnificent valleys, and a wealth of graceful lakes and rivers. The Swiss are independent, sophisticated, dignified and have a fierce loyalty to local districts claiming first to be Ticinese, Appenzellers, etc. and second, Swiss. They aim to preserve their cultural heritage and with reason are very proud of their homeland. Switzerland is wonderful and unique. It is a land where yodelers harmonize with cow bells.

For centuries Switzerland's beauty has inspired poets and artists who have advertised her glories on paper and canvas. Her reputation has attracted tourists from all over the world. Travelers come to explore her land and experience her culture. Challenged by her physical attributes perhaps, it was the sportsmen who first appreciated and came to this land of natural beauty and strength. Switzerland has the gift of the lakes and mountains; *"the palaces of nature"*, as stated by Byron.

It was a young Englishman, Edward Whymper who, on July 14 1865 at the age of twenty, conquered the most inaccessible of all mountains, the Matterhorn. What he described about Switzerland's mountains, holds true for the rest of the country, and expresses the essence of travel.

"However magnificent dreams of the imagination may be, they always remain inferior to reality.".

PURPOSE OF THIS GUIDE

I sincerely believe that SWISS COUNTRY INNS & CHALETS is, overall, the best book yet to appear in my series of travel guides. It reflects not just the experiences and input of one person, but the creative involvement of many. Long hours of research, travel, writing and evaluation have been dedicated with the intention to provide the traveler with the most accurate and comprehensive guide of its kind. A list of hotels and regions to be investigated was composed before ever leaving the United States. Guides already published were the principal source for those selections. However, it became dramatically obvious as we followed the path of their suggestions that a number of the places had never been personally visited by the authors. As a result, we made a number of detours in search of the advertised "perfect" inn, only to discover that its physical description did not match the written one. We were often disappointed and yet had allocated time for just such occurrences. It made us realize just how important and valuable a dependable list of hotels and suggested itineraries would be for the traveler who, in a restricted time frame, would want to relax and enjoy, not investigate. We returned with the determination to provide a guide whose list of hotels would include only ones that we had personally seen and whose suggested routings we had traveled.

We hope this guide will provide both vicarious pleasure for the armchair traveler and great practical assistance to the tourist who is packing his bags for a Swiss holiday. Most guides are written by travel writers. This book is written as part of an European Inn series by two travel consultants of Town and Country Travel Service in San Mateo, California. For years we have advised clients from behind our desk as to exactly how to plan and outline personal itineraries in an endeavor to make their holidays as pleasurable and memorable as possible. Our list of recommended hotels and itineraries are truly the result of our day by day profession. We have written this guide for our clients and friends.

HOTELS and RESTAURANTS

We offer you a list of inns with charm as the overall basis for their inclusion, though they may vary from luxurious and elegant to simple country cozy, and be found in cities, mountain villages or on remote country roads, they are all wonderful and all very Swiss. In a few instances, an inn has been chosen not on its merit alone, but because an area was so spectacular we felt it had to have a recommendation of a place to sojourn. We have endeavored through descriptions and by providing an illustration of each hotel to qualify and indicate the differences.

Regardless of the category of Swiss hotel, striving to achieve a high standard of service and quality of cuisine is generally stressed over the importance of the decor in the bedrooms. The old world charm is usually allocated to the public and dining areas, whereas the bedrooms are often simple and modern in their furnishings. From large hotels, where one might assume the owner to be insulated from the tedious day to day problems, to small inns, the dedication and personal involvement of the management is astounding. No job ever seems too small or inconsequential to merit attention. The hoteliers, many having studied in Switzerland's own prestigious hotel and restaurant schools, take great pride in their profession, and management is often passed down within a family from one generation to the next. It was wonderful to learn that many of the hoteliers' sons and daughters are now studying the trade so that there will be a continuity of this fine tradition.

It is not unusual to find the presence of the hoteliers both in the supervision of the hotel and the restaurant. It was more often than not that we would discover the owner in the kitchen, dusting flour off his apron before extending a welcome handshake! Switzerland boasts some of Europe's most outstanding restaurants. A great degree of professionalism and excellence is maintained in even the simplest of restaurants, and the presentation and quality of food would rival any of our city's finest. Expected only in the most exclusive, expensive restaurants in the United States, food exquisitely served, piping hot from a cart is a frequent occurrence in Switzerland. When finished, not only are you presented with a comparable second portion, it is brought to you on a clean warm plate with the same skillful delivery. Not once did I see a steam table. Vegetables were right from the garden. There seemed to always be a marvelous selection of fresh fish from the rivers and lakes, outstanding veal dishes, and wicked desserts followed by an assortment of local cheeses and seasonal fruits. To perfectly complement the meal, Switzerland produces some exceptional wines that are rarely exported - a definite loss to the rest of the world.

Most inns have at least two restaurants. Frequently there is a central entry hall with a somewhat "formal" restaurant on one side and a "pub-like", informal restaurant on the other. The latter is called the "stubli", and if you are in the countryside this is where the farmers gather in the late afternoon for a bit of farm gossip and perhaps a card game of "jass". Locals gather after work in the stubli for relaxation, and in the evening families congregate for a glass of beer, wine, a thimble full of Kirsch Schnapps, or a popular "spritzer".

SUPPLEMENTAL LIST OF HOTELS

Since our return from Switzerland, Swiss friends have kindly recommended a few additional inns. We debated a long time whether or not to consider the hotels for inclusion. It wasn't that we didn't value these recommendations, but rather we hesitated to recommend inns that we had not personally inspected. From brochures, however, they did look marvelous and so, rather than exclude them from this guide, we decided to include them in a special supplemental listing. Before the next edition we hope to have the opportunity to visit each of them. We do want to thank our wonderful Swiss friends for sharing with us some of their favorites! We want to extend a special thanks to our friend Jacqueline Walpoth who added so much "icing" to this book. Familiar with almost all of the hotels on our list, Jacqueline added little tidbits of local color, anecdotes about the owners and details of favorite restaurant entrees. Jacqueline also proved to be an invaluable final critic since her heart and home are Switzerland.

HOTEL RATES AND INFORMATION

Following each hotel description is an illustration and details concerning the hotel. Everything is self-expanatory but we thought it important to expand on the following few inclusions.

Hotel rates included are for rooms on a double occupancy basis. Wanting to offer you the most accurate rates, we have contacted the hotels directly, requesting the most current tariffs possible. However, individual hotel situations change and we include the rates, not as a direct quotation, but with the intention that they will be used only as a guideline. However, it is a pleasure to note that because inflation in Switzerland is very low, the hotel rates usually increase very little each year. Compared to other countries the rates are very stable - usually augmented by only about five percent annually.

We also mention whether or not a hotel will accept *credit cards* and specify which cards they will honor. They are noted in an abbreviated form as follows: AMERICAN EXPRESS = AE; BANK AMERICARD / VISA = VS; MASTER CHARGE = MC; DINERS CLUB = DC; EUROCARD = EC.

Hotel Representatives can prove invaluable and save both time and money when making reservations. Located in the United States they represent specific hotels or chain of hotels, and can advise you as to the status of availability for a specific date, room rates, and are able to assist you in co-ordinating hotel reservations to complement your itinerary. For the first time in one of my guides, I refer to Hotel Representatives where applicable and provide a telephone contact.

HOTEL RESERVATIONS

With luck you might be able to just "drop in" at some of the hotels described in this guide and secure a room, but during the tourist season most hotels need a prior reservation. Therefore, if you can structure your holiday in advance I strongly suggest prior reservations. Reservations are especially important in Switzerland for several reasons. First, hotel space in the major cities such as Zurich, Lucerne, Geneva, and Basel is usually *very* scarce. Even in "off season" the cities are frequently booked solid with conventions and it is sometimes impossible to secure a room. Second, during the tourist season the country inns are usually very busy with the Swiss themselves who love to escape to the mountains with their families for a hiking holiday. Third, many of the hotels in this guide are in remote areas and it would be terribly frustrating to arrive in some hamlet after hours of driving to find the only inn already filled. Here are several suggestions for making reservations:

DIRECT PHONE CALL: Telephone numbers including area codes are given in this guide. Usually you can dial direct. Check with your local long distance operator for rates and instructions. If time is at a premium this is certainly the most efficient method. If you time your call to the off-peak hours the cost is not great.

LETTER: If you have ample time, a letter can be an inexpensive way to request hotel space. Allow four weeks minimum time for an answer to your letter. A letter written in English is usually adequate because most Swiss hoteliers can read

English even if they are not fluent in English. Europeans frequently reverse the month and date, so be sure to write the name of the month instead of using a number. To avoid confusion, it is best to state your date of arrival and your date of departure. Clearly tell how many persons are in your party, how many rooms you desire, and if you want a private bathroom. Ask for the rates and how much deposit is needed to secure the reservation.

TRAVEL AGENCY: A travel agent can be a great asset in "tying" together all of the threads of your holiday. A knowledgeable agent can be of tremendous assistance too in sorting through the jungle of airline fares and routing possibilities and helping you choose the best. When a travel agent writes your transportation ticket there is usually no fee since travel consultants work as agents for airlines, ships, and trains. However, most travel agents do charge a service fee when making hotel reservations because so much time is involved in correspondence, deposit checks, acceptance letters, and vouchers. But for a busy person, the assistance given and time saved when using the services of a travel consultant is often money well spent. Choose a travel agent who is knowledgeable, easy to work with, and reputable. Be frank about your budget and expectations. Be candid about asking in advance as to service charges to avoid misunderstandings.

TELEX: Some of the hotels in this guide have telex numbers which are included in the hotel information section. If you have access to a telex machine this is a very efficient way to request accommodations. Be very specific as to your date of arrival and date of departure, type of rooms desired, number of rooms needed, and number of people in your party. Also, be sure to include your return telex number.

U.S. REPRESENTATIVE: Some hotels have a United States representative. We have listed the names of the representatives and the telephone numbers in the information section of the hotels.

FOOD SPECIALTIES

Switzerland is bordered by Germany, Austria, Italy and France and has the advantage of absorbing specialties of each of her neighbors into the Swiss kitchen. The genius of the Swiss chefs interprets these various foods into gourmet delights.

Many guide books infer that the Swiss cooking is mediocre - that it has no character or style of its own. I feel that this is totally unfair. Probably due to the high degree of training stressed in the Swiss hotel schools, you will find consistently superb food and service from the famous, deluxe restaurants in the cities to the simple, tiny restaurants in remote hamlets.

I am not going to attempt to list all of the Swiss specialities. Instead I will give you a sampling of some of the delicacies I most enjoyed while in Switzerland. I will leave the joy of completing the list to your culinary adventures.

CHEESES: Switzerland is famous for her cheeses. Appenzell and Gruyeres are both fabulous Swiss cheeses that I especially enjoyed.

RACLETTE: Raclette is a fun cheese dish. A block of Bagnes Cheese is split and melted over a fire. The softened cheese is scraped off onto your plate and eaten with potatoes and onions.

FONDUE: The Swiss specialty of fondue has gained popularity all over the world. Melted Gruyeres cheese, white wine, garlic, and kirsch are brought hot to the table in a chaffing dish and the diners use long forks to dip squares of bread into the delectable mixture.

ROSCHTI: All over Switzerland the delicious fried potatoes called "Roschti" are served.

GESCHNETZLETS: Veal is very popular in Switzerland. Perhaps the most famous and delicious method of preparation is small pieces cooked in a white wine sauce with mushrooms. This is frequently called "Veal Zurich" on the menu.

BUNDNERFLEISCH: In southeastern Switzerland, the Grisons area, an unusual air dried beef cut into wafer thin slices is served as a delicacy.

FRITURE DE PERCHETTES: Nothing could be more superb than the tiny, mild filet of fresh perch fried in butter found on most of the menus during the summer in the Lake Geneva area. Be sure to try this outstanding gourmet delight!

BRATWURSTE: I am sure the Swiss would laugh to see me include such a common fare as Bratwurste in my specialty food list! However, there is nothing more delicious than the plump grilled veal Swiss "hot dogs" smothered in onions and accompanied by fried potatoes. A cold beer makes this meal paradise.

LECKERLI: This is a spicy, cake-like, ginger flavored cookie covered with a thin sugar icing. To be really "good" it must "snap" when broken.

HERO JAM: This divine jam comes in many delicious fruit and berry flavors and is traditionally served with little hard rolls that break into quarters. The texture and flavor of Hero Jam is so magnificent that I am sure you would swear it came from Grandmother's kitchen!

CHOCOLATE: This list would not be complete without the mention of Swiss Chocolate! Nestle, Chocolat Tobler, or simply "Swiss" are synonymous with some of the world's best chocolate. Not one suitcase returns to the States without a bar or two tucked into the corner!

ITINERARIES

We have included five itineraries for Switzerland, each highlighting the entire country rather than a particular region and each designed around an individual theme. *SWISS HIGHLIGHTS* is written for the first time traveler to Switzerland. It is an introduction to the major cities and popular destinations. *MOUNTAIN ADVENTURES* explores some of Switzerland's most spectacular mountain villages and settings. *MEDIEVAL VILLAGES* traces a journey through some of Switzerland's most enchanting walled towns and medieval villages. Saturated with history and a romantic past, this itinerary steps into an era of knights, chivalry, castles, cobblestoned streets, wenches, jousting, jesters, turrets, bows and arrows. *BEST ON A BUDGET* was created for a friend, for anyone young at heart and traveling on a budget, and for those who seek the traditional Swiss inns and yet appreciate it when the simplicity of accommodation is reflected in the price. It highlights some beautiful little villages that merit a stay of a few days, but might not otherwise have been included because the selection of inns was limited to simple, family style hotels. *SWITZERLAND: BY TRAIN, BOAT AND BUS* takes advantage of the country's fantastic transportation network and lets you most effectively soak in the splendors of its valleys, mountains, rivers and lakes without having to attempt the roads and passes in your own car. Most of Switzerland's highlights are incorporated into the itinerary and routing is determined by the most romantic and picturesque means of travel.

These itineraries, with the exception of *SWITZERLAND: BY TRAIN, BOAT AND BUS*, are designed for touring Switzerland by car. There is no comparable way to travel, to explore the countryside, to really understand the depths and reaches of a valley, to fully comprehend the dimensions, magnificence and power of its lofty alpine peaks, and to experience the beauty and grace of its lakes and rivers. Cars are easy to rent and available in most mid-sized towns and driving is on the "proper" side. The roads, like everything else in Switzerland, are professionally marked and once you get used to the excellent color-coded sign system, directions are easy to follow. Green signs depict freeways. Blue signs mark regular roads. White signs depict the smaller roads. Yellow signs mark walking paths or roads closed to vehicle traffic. Most of the roads are excellent, but some of the smaller roads in remote areas or over narrow, twisting mountain passes are not recommended for the feint of heart or hesitant drivers. It is also necessary to note that certain mountain passes close during winter months and it wise to route accordingly. However, to accommodate the winter season, Switzerland boasts some of the world's most impressive mountain passes and tunnels. While driving in Switzerland it is also wise to know that there is a road condition hotline reached by dialing 163.

A map at the beginning of each itinerary outlines its route and details suggested sightseeing and overnight stops. The maps are intended to serve only as a guideline. To supplement this book and simplify your own travels, we suggest that you use and refer to some excellent road maps. We personally prefer Michelin maps, which are very detailed and consistently accurate. The maps highlight in green the most scenic routes. Michelin is also the only map we found to have a city index enabling you to pin point any destination. The other advantage to Michelin maps is that they cross reference beautifully with their publications of regional sightseeing guides.

As it is not always easy to locate good maps, we recommend *Forsyth Travel Library* as an excellent and very reliable source. If you call or contact them by mail they will send you a catalog of maps and books and often can accommodate special requests or items not advertised on the list. Their address is: *Forsyth Travel Library, Post Office Box 2975, 9154 West 57th Street, Shawnee Mission, Kansas 66201* and telephone number is: *(913) 384-3440*.

ALTERNATE MEANS OF TRANSPORTATION

Although cars afford the flexibility to deviate on a whim and explore enticing side roads or beckoning hilltop villages, Switzerland's transportation network is so extensive it can be traveled conveniently by train, boat or bus and seen from the largest city to the smallest hamlet. Similar in principal to the Eurail Pass, the *HOLIDAY CARD* is an incredible value if you are traveling exclusively in Switzerland. It gives a choice of first or second class and enables travel for periods of four, eight, fifteen or thirty days on all trains of the Swiss Federal Railways , on nearly all private railways as well as lake steamers and postbuses. It also enables travel at a reduced rate on many mountain railways and cable cars. The card must be purchased outside Switzerland through travel agents, Swissair, or any Swiss National Tourist Office, and is not available to Swiss residents. Also available, but exclusively for the bus systems, are *POST ROVER* tickets which qualify for seven days of unlimited travel.

Trains ⟨⊕⟩ SBB

Switzerland has one of the most remarkable rail systems in the world with more than 3,400 miles of track, just over half are operated by the Swiss Federal Railway system, the others are privately owned. However they are all integrated and connections are scheduled to synchronize both efficiently and conveniently. Their time table is patterned after the perfection of the Swiss Clock . With train departures to the second, the maintaining of schedules is almost humorous.

The train stations, often chalet-style buildings, are spotlessly clean, and many times double as a residence for the station master. The buildings are charming in their Swiss architecture. The evidence of domesticity with flowers cascading from the upstairs window boxes and laundry hanging on the line is frequently evident. The station masters are always handsome in their "toy" uniforms and most speak some English.

Buses

Boasting more mileage than the Swiss railway itself, the Postal Bus lines originated after World War I with the primary purpose to transport mail.In conjunction with the entire network of railway lines, every village in Switzerland is serviced, and as buses are also available for public use, theyprovide Switzerland with one of the most exceptional transportation networks in the world. Depending on the demand, under the auspices of the postal bus line, are four to five person limousines, mini-buses or the ever familiar yellow buses. In addition to the mail, the bus lines are responsible for transporting about fifteen million passengers and their dependability and excellence of service are extremely impressive.

Maneuvering the roads and passes of Switzerland, the postal bus drivers are unmatched in their ability and skills. Their record is faultless. In the history of their service there has not been one fatal accident nor have they been responsible for any minor mishaps. Their work is deemed one of the mostglamorous in the country and in the villages they play an important role in the community. Usually they are well versed on the local news and social activities and familiar with the most recent wedding, gossip or current business venture. Their position is prestigious but also well deserved and earned. They literally "know every millimeter" of the road and the training they endure is exacting and stringent. Thousands apply each year for positions available to just a few. To qualify for consideration alone is demanding and selective. An applicant must be no older than twenty-eight; have had at least four years experience as a mechanic; have trained for a year as a truck driver; have completed his military duty; and be able to speak three languages. If they then pass a rigorous physical exam they commence with years of specialized training before taking position behind the wheel. They are first assigned for several years to drive a postal truck and then a bus in the lowlands. As a finale they must negotiate a bus up a treacherous mountain road, extremely narrow with a number of hairpin turns and then successfully complete a seemingly impossible U-turn, all to be observed and judged not by one examiner but by a bus load of veteran bus drivers! Justifiably, those who achieve position as postal driver, have command of the roadways and other vehicles are expected to yield. It is not uncommon to view a bus driver assisting a petrified driver who has understandably encountered difficulty on a pass or narrow bend and who is too frightened to move!

To ride the postal buses is to observe some of the world's most critical and acclaimed drivers and to truly experience the ability of the Swiss transportation network. As the buses wind up the incredible mountain passes the sound of their horn, warning other vehicles of their approach, is familiar and fun. As is their logo, the postal horn is reminiscent of the days of yore and plays a tune from Rossini's "William Tell Overture".

Boats

Switzerland is a land of lakes and rivers and to travel the country by its waterways affords an entirely new and enchanting perspective. Often a river boat or lake steamer will depart from a dock just a few feet from a hotel enabling you to journey from one destination to another or continue inland by connecting with either a train, bus or hired car. Concerned with preserving their heritage, the Swiss are also responsible for providing the necessary funding to refurbish a number of the beautiful and graceful lake steamers and ferries. Not only can you see Switzerland by water but also experience some nostalgia.

Fly Rail

One of the greatest advantages of using the Swiss transportation network is the convenient handling of luggage. Only in a country as dependable and efficient as Switzerland would you dare to check your luggage at a travel counter and expect to see it in a reasonable period of time at the specified destination! Often you will be surprised to have your luggage actually arrive before you, and awaiting your arrival.

Given a choice between the Zurich and Geneva airport, my preference would be Zurich, as trains depart from its basement almost hourly to every region in Switzerland. The railway station with its ticket and reservation counter, information center, foreign exchange, and luggage registration office is located next to Terminal B. You can check your luggage from the station or be free of it even earlier by checking it from a desk that is situated in the arrival hall, just to the left as you clear customs, to any Swiss railway or postal bus station and many of the boat docks. For an unbelievably low cost there is no more struggling with baggage enroute! In fact if you have reservations at a hotel convenient to the train, bus station or boat dock, if you provide the management with your claim check you might pleasantly find that a porter will retrieve it and deliver it directly to your room. By arranging to have your luggage sent straight from the airport to your hotel is not only a luxury it also saves on tips as there will only be the hotel porter to tip as opposed to the man at the airport, at the train or bus station and then at the hotel. How wonderful and feasible only in Switzerland!

When it is time to return home, the Swiss have devised an even more impressive handling of luggage. From over one hundred train or postal coach stations throughout Switzerland you can check your luggage via the Geneva or Zurich airport all the way to your own home town airport! They call it *"FLY LUGGAGE"*. All you need is a plane ticket for any scheduled flight from Zurich or Geneva with a confirmed reservation. The nominal cost is per piece of luggage. If you have a railway ticket to the Zurich or Geneva airports you pay even less.

 **A LITTLE BIT ABOUT THE SWISS**

The Swiss call their country Helvetia. All Federal documents bear the seal of the Confederatio Helvetica, CH, or Swiss Confederation. Their flag dates from the thirteenth century. In 1863 the International Red Cross, to honor its Swiss founder, adopted the banner with colors reversed. Swiss independence dates to the days of William Tell when the magistrates from three cantons, then under Hapsburg rule, met to courageously and successfully oppose the hand of the ruling landholders. It was in 1291, on a meadow near Lake Lucerne, at the Rutli, that the magistrates set seal to the Confederation Helvetica. Those original three cantons, Uri, Schwyz and Unterwalden have expanded over the centuries into twenty-five, (twenty-two if you do not consider the semi-cantons of Appenzell, Basel and Unterwalden). Each of the twenty-five cantons guards its autonomy and separate identity. The canton of Berne is the capital of Switzerland and serves as the seat of the Federal Government. However, the Swiss have historically shunned centralization of power and so rather than have too many federal branches in one city, they cautiously maintain supreme court at Lausanne.

Switzerland is a small country, barely two hundred miles wide and one hundred miles north to south, it has a compulsory military service, determined to protect its hard won independence, national character and peace. Every young Swiss man must enlist at the age of twenty and complete seventeen weeks of basic training. Then until the age of fifty or fifty-five he is responsible for participating in a few weeks of annual "refresher" courses. Their military force is always ready to defend the country and can be coordinated into action on a moment's notice. Often we encountered such training groups who were "stationed" at our hotel. They would practice maneuvers by day to return to the hotel in the late afternoon and spend their leisure hours often washing their Mercedes. The most humorous example of their presence, however, was at night when we would retire and find heavy combat boots lining the hall, left out to be polished. Where else but in Switzerland!

PEOPLE

Contrary to what I had heard about the Swiss being aloof and unfriendly, I found them to be very cordial, warm, and hospitable. Not a back slapping friendliness, but a friendliness with reserve and dignity - no less real while contained in the realm of "proper". The Swiss do not have an immediate first name, folksy hospitality...rather a genuine warmth and caring. Perhaps the Swiss dedication to hard work, their total  responsibility to provide excellence of service, and their respect for privacy has been misinterpreted as "coldness". Once you become their friend and they do not feel they will be invading your privacy, they are extremely charming and gracious.

LANGUAGE

Switzerland is a country of several official languages. Switzerland does not have its own language - the closest they come to their own language might be Romanish which is spoken by a small number of people in south eastern Switzerland. The other major languages are French, Germany, and Italian. German is the dominant language and is spoken all over central and northern Switzerland. Italian is spoken in the south and French is spoken in the west. English is usually spoken in the hotels and shops of tourist centers. When you are in remote areas you might need to communicate with a dictionary and a smile.

SHOPPING

Switzerland has a tempting array of specialities to entice even the reluctant shopper. Shopping in Switzerland is fun; the shops are so pretty and the merchandise usually is of excellent quality. While in Zurich do not overlook a marvelous store near the *Zum Storchen Hotel* that has an exceptional selection of art and handcraft items. It is called Schweizer Heimatwerk. In Switzerland the prices are usually set so there is no bargaining. The tax is normally included in the price. However, there is a tax free town, Samnaun, located in a remote corner of eastern Switzerland near the Austrian border. Here unbelieveable prices and a fantastic assortment of items attract shoppers from all over Europe.

Following are some shopping suggestions: *WATCHES & CLOCKS, MECHANICAL TOYS, WOOD CARVINGS, SWISS ARMY KNIVES, CHOCOLATES, CHEESES, KIRSCH SCHNAPPS, ANTIQUES, ST GALLEN LACE, HAND EMBROIDERED ITEMS, FINE COTTON MATERIAL, CHILDREN'S CLOTHING, SKI WEAR.*

SPORTS

Sports are an integral part of the lure of Switzerland. The mountains have been tempting adventurers to Switzerland since the middle of the 1800's when Edward Whymper crossed the channel from England to be the first to reach the top of the famous Matterhorn.

The whole of Switzerland is like a gorgeous park - a paradise for the sportsman! The fame of the ski areas such as Zermatt, St. Moritz, Davos, Wengen, Klosters, Villars and Verbier has spread throughout the world. The glory of the mountain lakes such as Lake Geneva, Lake Lucerne, and Lake Zurich are ideal for boating, fishing and swimming. The reputation of the incredible array of marked walking trails has beckoned hikers from far and near.

GEOGRAPHY

Switzerland is very special because of her unique geography. The impression is a country of dramatic physical beauty.

In the north western section of Switzerland are the Jura mountains. To the south east sixty percent is dominated by the gorgeous Alps. In between these two mountainous areas the verdant lowlands sweep from Lake Geneva diagonally across the country to Lake Constance.

The impression one returns home with is of precipitous alpine peaks, deep mountain gorges, narrow mountain valleys, glaciers gleaming in the sun fighting the ravages of time, beautiful rushing streams, glorious blue lakes, gently flowing rivers, low timberlines, spectacular water falls, and soft rolling hills. Switzerland is truly a photographer's paradise. Every turn in the road offers a "post card" vista for your scrapbook of memories.

WEATHER

Switzerland is a country of many climates. The high mountain weather is unlike the milder climate around Lake Geneva. The Lake Geneva area is unlike the balmy Italian Lake district. The central valleys have a climate all their own. The tourist season extends almost all year in Switzerland. The only exceptions perhaps would be November when the glory of winter has not yet arrived and the colorful fall season has subsided or in March when winter is losing its splendor and blossoms of Spring have not yet appeared.

Winter is the season for the sports enthusiasts with excellent downhill ski slopes, beautifully marked cross country trails, skating, and curling. Winter is also for those who simply love the charm of picture book villages wrapped in blankets of snow. Many roads are closed in the winter so your route should be carefully planned.

Summer is the most popular season. The days are usually mild and sunny and the mountain passes are open so you can explore all the isolated little villages.

Spring is my favorite time of year. Weather in late spring can be absolutely glorious. The meadows are a symphony of color with a profusion of wildflowers. The fields are brilliant green and the mountains still have their winter cap of snow.

Fall is also a good time to visit Switzerland. The first snow storms leave the mountains wearing new bonnets of pristine snow. The trees and vineyards are mellowing in shades of red and gold. The flowers are at their peak of bloom in every window box. There is a hint of winter in the air except in the southern Italian lake district where the weather is usually still balmy.

A note of advice concerning the weather. As you admire the green fields, their very lushness suggests that it frequently rains in Switzerland. It is hard to predict when it will rain - weather is truly a matter of luck. So do not set your heart on all sunny days. The chances are that you will have some rain and some sun. Be prepared in heart and rain apparel, and rest assured - you will love Switzerland rain or shine.

SWISS NATIONAL TOURIST OFFICE

The Swiss have earned themselves the reputation as very "proper" and gracious. Our experiences proved only to exemplify those very qualities during our travels and on the occasion of meeting Mr Willy Isler, manager of the Swiss National Tourist Office in San Francisco. He has given generously of his time and shared with us tales of his own travels. We thank Mr Willy Isler and his staff for their infectious love of their country and genuine interest in our book. They have been of great assistance to us and can prove invaluable should you need information or advice when planning your own Swiss vacation.

Switzerland

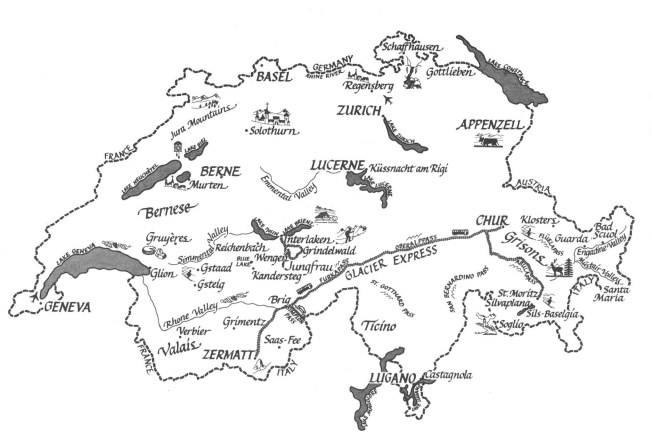

Sightseeing Reference for Itineraries

The five suggested itineraries in this guide criss cross back and forth across Switzerland describing routes tailored for individual whims and budgets. Because certain "key" towns reappear in several itineraries we decided to have an individual sightseeing section as a quick reference of what to expect along your route. The following towns, listed alphabetically, appear in the itineraries as overnight destinations.

APPENZELL

Appenzell is a "picture book perfect" village. The town is justifiably famous with tourists who flock to see the marvelous designs painted on the facades of the buildings, a colorful variety of artwork - landscapes, folk art, flowers, abstract designs, animals, and people, Appenzell is famous also for the local exquisite embroidery and delicious cheeses.

Politically, Appenzell is well known for its demonstration of real democracy! On the last Sunday in April, the citizens, usually wearing their colorful traditional costumes, gather in the town square to elect the representatives to their local Canton. This is done with a show of hands.

The most appealing aspect of Appenzell is not Appenzell itself, but rather the glorious countryside which surrounds it. This area of Switzerland is magnificent with lush, rolling, gentle green fields accented with plump, happy cows lazily munching grass to the rhythm of their cow bells. Snuggled in these lovely pastures are magnificent farmhouses. Not little chalets, but huge structures where the family's home, adorned with masses of flowers, is attached to the barn where the animals are within easy access during the snows of winter. The total effect of this idyllic farm area is one of tranquil beauty.

BASEL

The town of Basel is well worth a visit. It is an industrial city, the second largest in Switzerland. From the outskirts, the city is not very attractive, but when you arrive at the heart of the old town, you will find a delightful medieval city - a very real city functioning as a center for banking, insurance, trade and commerce. Being at the border of France and Germany and linked by the Rhine with central Europe, Basel has a very important strategic location. The Rhine acts as the gateway to the North Sea, so Basel is also a very busy port.

The old town is beautifully preserved and it is delightful to stroll the back streets and discover wonderful little squares and colorful fountains tucked away. In the old town you will want to visit the Cathedral which dates back to the twelfth century. Also in your wanderings you will come across the Market Square (Markplatz) which is host every morning to a flower and vegetable market. The Town Hall (Rathaus) dates from the sixteenth century and is beautifully decorated with frescoes. If you enjoy museums, there is an excellent museum of Fine Arts (Kuntsmuseum) which features works of art of the fifteenth and sixteenth centuries. Another museum is the Museum of Antique Art (Antikenmuseum) which features sculptures and art dating from the pre-Hellenic times to the Roman era.

In summer there are boat tours which offer a leisurely view of the city. This method of sightseeing is especially interesting because from the river you can view many of the marvelous old buildings which line the river and also cross under some of the bridges which so colorfully span the Rhine.

BERNE

Berne is a beautifully preserved sixteenth century medieval city. It has a fascinating setting nestled on a hill which is almost completely encircled by a loop of the Aare River. Further enhancing the picture, the mountains rise in the background. The setting alone would make Berne worth a stop, but the town itself has lots of character and and interesting sightseeing attractions.

The Marktgasse, the main street of the old part of Berne, has charming medieval buildings, arcaded sidewalks, intriguing shops, and whimsical fountains.

My favorite attraction in Berne is the clock tower which until the thirteenth century was the town's West Gate. This clock tower appeals to the child in all of us. Four minutes before the hour the "show" begins that cannot help but bring a smile. As the bell peals, there is a succession of figures which parade across the clock including the most popular of all - darling little bear cubs.

Berne is an easy walking city. Just a stroll from the Clock tower is the Nydegg Bridge . From here you have wonderful views of the town and, if you are a photographer, some great shots.

CASTAGNOLA

Castagnola is a lake side community close to Lugano. From Castagnola there is a scenic walking path connecting Castagnola with the small town of Gandria. This trail hugs the shore of Lake Lugano and makes a wonderful excursion on a nice day. To add to the enjoyment, you can stop along the way at one of the little lake front cafes for refreshment. However, Castagnola's real claim to fame in the "sightseeing department" is the *VILLA FAVORITA*. What luck for the tourist that in the tiny town of Castagnola is one of the finest museums in Switzerland! The museum is located in a parklike setting in a beautiful mansion on the shore of the lake and contains many masterpieces by European artists. Since this is a private museum check carefully at your hotel to find out what hours it is open.

GENEVA

Geneva is frequently thought of as a "new" city - a city of banking and commerce; an international city housing the Place Des Nations; a city of beautiful shops; a city of museums and culture; an industrial city. All this is true, but Geneva also has one of the most attractive medieval sections in Switzerland. "Old Geneva" is located on the south side of the Rhone River. Here the hills rise steeply from the shore of the lake and the streets twist and turn in a maze of fascinating little shops, fountains, flower filled squares, and charming buildings. This area is crowned by St. Peter's Cathedral which dominates the old town. The Cathedral, constructed in the twelfth century, is usually open daily. Within the church is a triangular chair supposedly the one used by Calvin, and also the tomb of Duc De Rohn who was the leader of the French Protestants during the time of Henri IV. But perhaps the most spectacular part of the St. Peter's Cathedral is the climb to the top of the north tower where you will have a spectacular view of Geneva and beyond to the lake and the majestic backdrop of the alps. Also in the old town, you might want to see the town hall which dates from the sixteenth century. After visiting St. Peter's, wander down the little twisting streets exploring small antique shops and back alleys. You cannot get lost because it is all downhill and when you are at the bottom, you are at the lake! There is a park along the banks of the lake - notice in the park a clock made out of flowers!

On the north side of the Rhone River circling around the lake is the newer section of Geneva. In this area there are lovely lake promenades with gorgeous flowers, stately hotels, small squares, and fancy shops. This too is a wonderful "strolling" part of the city - especially in early spring when the tulips are incredibly beautiful. However, you will see lovely flowers in the parks at all seasons except in the winter.

Geneva has many museums and interesting sightseeing destinations. The *PALAIS DES NATIONS* is open daily except when conferences are convening and during special holidays. Usually, however, like many museums, it is closed for a few hours in the middle of the day. There are many guided tours. The palace is located in the Park De L'Ariana and was the headquarters of the League of Nations. Now it is the seat of the European·branch of the United Nations. The *PETIT PALAIS MUSEUM* is open daily except Monday mornings and holidays. This museum is in a mansion and features French painters from the end of the impressionistic period. The *MUSEUM OF OLD MUSICAL INSTRUMENTS* displays a wonderful collection of European musical instruments. Since you are in

Switzerland, the home of the clock, you might want to visit the *WATCH and CLOCK MUSEUM* with displays of time pieces from their origin to the present day.

You really cannot help loving Geneva with its sophisticated beauty and international air. As you meander the parks and promenades, you could be anywhere in the world. You see all nationalities and hear all languages. This is a city we all seem to love and share.

GLION

Glion is a small town located in the hills high above Montreux. Because of its superb location with a panorama of Lake Geneva and the mountains, Glion has attracted the wealthy who have built beautiful mansions nestled among the trees. You can reach Glion by car, or if arriving from Geneva by boat, there is a tram connecting the dock at Territet with Glion. There is also a train from Montreux to Glion.

Glion's main attraction is the view, however, just a short distance away, located on Lake Geneva, is the *CASTLE OF CHILLON* - made famous by Lord Byron's famous poem. This castle is well worth a visit. It has a fantastic setting on a small rock jutting into the lake. Walking over a bridge, you enter the Castle of Chillon where you can visit the torture chamber plus many rooms with excellent medieval furnishings.

GOTTLIEBEN

Gottlieben is located on the Rhine just before it enters Lake Constance. The town is of special interest because of its two famous hotels - the Krone and the Drachenburg & Waaghaus - picturesquely situated on the banks of the river. From Gottlieben you can take ferry boats down the Rhine to Stein am Rhein and Schaffhausen or you can travel by boat through the channels into Lake Constance.

GRIMENTZ

Grimentz is a delightful little village snuggled on a plateau at the end of Anniviers valley which stretches south from the Rhone Valley. Like other Swiss towns retaining so much of their original charm, the government protects the architectural standards. This is a town of small Valais-style wooden houses darkened almost black with age, usually with a slate roof and suspended above the ground on stone pillars. My guess is that the Grimentz of old actually could never be as lovely as it is today for each resident seems to vie with his neighbor for the most magnificent display of brilliant red geraniums. On a sunny day the effect is glorious - brilliant blue sky, snow-capped mountains, green pastures, and antique little homes exploding in geraniums.

GRINDELWALD

Grindelwald captures for many the romanticized image of Switzerland. It is a charming alpine village sprawled on a lovely expanse of meadows and surrounded by magnificent towering mountains. It is a popular destination for exploring the Jungfrau range for it is as close as you can come by car to view the spectacular giants of the Jungfrau region: the Eiger rising to 13,026 ft., the Wetterhorn to 12,143 ft. and the Mettenberg to 10,184 ft. From the little station in town the train departs for the dramatic Kleine Scheidegg and on to the Jungfraujoch. *Please refer to JUNGFRAU sightseeing.*

GRUYERES

Gruyeres is a beautiful little medieval village nestled on top of a tiny mountain just north of Lake Geneva and south of Berne. This is such a unique and charming little town that it is considered a national monument and its architectural purity is protected by the Swiss government. Cars are not allowed into the village but there are several parking lots strategically located on the road which winds up from the valley to the town. Another bonus for Gruyeres, as you probably guessed from the name of the town, is its location in the center of one of Switzerland's famous dairy areas...the cheeses and creams are marvelous. Stop for a famous Gruyeres quiche, or if in season, fresh berries and cream - fantastic!

Gruyeres is a convenient town to use as a headquarters for a few days. The countryside in summer is exactly what one dreams about as being truly "Switzerland". The meadows are incredibly green. Lazy cows with tinkling bells lazily graze in the pastures, wildflowers abound in the fields, window boxes full of bright geraniums adorn the houses, all enhanced by the painted backdrop of gorgeous mountains.

One short excursion is to the small museum-factory just at the bottom of the hill as you drive down from Gruyeres. This is a modern building which you really can't miss as it has the entire outside wall painted with a pastoral scene. In the factory you can see how cheeses are made in Switzerland in the various cantons and also watch an English version movie explaining the process. Also, if you are a cheese enthusiast you can make short excursions to visit some of the other little villages in the area and sample their dairy products...You might come home a little plumper, but a connoisseur of the delicious Swiss cheeses.

The secret to discovering the fairy tale enchantment of Gruyeres is to spend the night here so that the town is *yours* in the hushed morning and the still hours of dusk. Leave mid day when the tour buses deposit their eager load of tourists to return late in the day, to sit on the terrace and to have a quiet drink listening to the tinkling of cow bells and watching the meadows soften in the fading sunlight.

GSTAAD

In spite of the fact that Gstaad has an international reputation as a very chic ski resort catering to the wealthy jet-set, the town retains much of its old world, small town, charming simplicity. In fact, in summer you might well be awakened by the wonderful medley of cowbells as the herds are driven out to pasture. The setting of Gstaad is magnificent with rugged mountain peaks rising steeply on each side of the valley. In summer the hiking or mountain climbing is excellent. In winter Gstaad offers one of the most famous network of ski trails in Switzerland

GSTEIG

Just a few miles beyond Gstaad is the picturesque hamlet of Gsteig which shares the same pretty mountain valley as its fancy neighbor yet is quainter and less expensive. Being a little village, Gsteig does not offer the luxury shops nor the extensive selection of restaurants as the internationally famous Gstaad. However, for those of you who prefer an unspoilt farming village, complete with beautifully carved chalets and a marvelous little church, Gsteig might be perfect.

GUARDA

Guarda has a spectacular location perched high on a ledge overlooking the Engadine Valley. The main "recreation" here is being out of doors exploring the beautiful mountain paths and soaking up the sensational beauty of the mountain peaks. However, there is some "formal" sightseeing which can be included in your plans. Nearby is *TARASP CASTLE* which crowns a tiny mountain in the valley below Guarda. In addition to being extremely picturesque, there are guided tours of the castle during the summer months. Also near Guarda is the tiny town of Sent whose position on a terrace overlooking the valley is similar to that of Guarda. Sent is famous for its many fascinating old buildings decorated with intricate line drawings.

INTERLAKEN

For many years Interlaken has attracted tourists from all over the world who come to enjoy the unbeatable combination of two of the most beautiful lakes in Switzerland with some of her most glorious mountain peaks! Interlaken has a fabulous location on a spit of land connecting Lake Brienz and Lake Thun. The town has many grand Victorian style hotels and fancy shops and restaurants.

Interlaken's location makes it a prime destination for those who want to take the circle train excursion to enjoy the majestic summit of the Jungfrau. *Please refer to JUNGFRAU sightseeing* .

JUNGFRAU EXCURSION

The below diagram will demonstrate how the pieces of this travel "jig-saw" puzzle fits together and corresponds with the following text and explanation.

The Jungfrau excursion is one of the highlights of Switzerland, and one which is mentioned in four of the following itineraries. Although this is a very popular trip, unless you have traveled the route, it sounds quite complicated. It is not. But I will try to explain, step by step, how this fabulous mountain adventure is maneuvered to give you the confidence to do it on your own.

This is an expensive train excursion and since it is on private rail lines it is not included on your Eurail Pass nor the Swiss Rail Pass - however, on a clear day it is worth every penny.

The Jungfrau excursion is a series of little trains synchronized to provide you with a glorious prize - the summit of the Jungfrau. The most popular starting points for this outing are from any of the following train stations: *INTERLAKEN OST, LAUTERBRUNNEN, GRINDELWALD, or WENGEN.*

This trip is usually accomplished as a "circle trip" providing the maximum of mountain vistas. I am going to describe the complete circle for you with the idea that you can tailor the trip to suit your special needs beginning and ending at the town you have chosen to spend the night.

The complete circle usually begins at Interlaken Ost (Interlaken East) train station. Here you board the train for the twenty-five minute train ride to *LAUTERBRUNNEN.* At Lauterbrunnen you change trains for the forty-five minute ride up the mountain to *KLEINE SCHEIDEGG* (stopping enroute to pick up passengers at the little town of *WENGEN*) . It is necessary to change trains again at Kleine Scheidegg for the final assent of the Jungfrau. The last leg of your train adventure is an incredible fifty-five minutes in which the train creeps up the steep mountain and disappears within a four-mile tunnel - reappearing at the Jungfraubahn, the highest rail station in Europe. It is possible to take an elevator even higher through the mountain to a vista point. From here, on a clear day, it seems you can see the whole of Switzerland. There is also an ice palace carved into the glacier, dog sled rides, shops, post offices, restaurants, etc. For this journey, be sure to take sturdy shoes for walking on the glacier, gloves, a warm sweater or jacket and sun glasses.

When you leave the Jungfrau it is necessary for the first leg to retrace your journey to *KLEINE SCHEIDEGG*. For scenic variety, most prefer to return to Interlaken by a circle route. To do this board the train for *GRINDELWALD*. At Grindelwald you can connect with another train which will take you directly to Interlaken.

KANDERSTEG

Kandersteg is a hamlet nestled at the end of the Kandertal Valley. The road ends here so those who want to continue on across the mountain range for the "short cut" to the Rhone Valley must travel by train (if you are driving, it is at Kandersteg that you need to put your car on the train for the "piggy - back" ride through the mountain.) But Kandersteg is far more than a train depot - this is a lovely little mountain village with a stupendous back drop of majestic mountains, a paradise for mountain lovers.

KLOSTERS

The town of Klosters "backs up" to the same mountains as Davos and actually the two ski areas interconnect like a giant spider web. Although much of Klosters is newly constructed in response to the need for tourist accommodations the town has grown with a gracious style encompassing the Swiss chalet motif. There are many lovely shops and restaurants. The town is also very well situated for hiking in the summer or skiing in the winter. The train station is the terminus for a cableway which rises high above the village to the marvelous ski runs. Also, popular in winter are tobogganing, cross country skiing, curling, and ice skating. But my favorite time for Klosters is the summer when the fields are vibrant with wild flowers and the majestic mountains stand guard over this lovely little town.

KUSSNACHT am RIGI

Sometimes there is confusion about the location of Kussnacht am Rigi because there is a town with a very similar spelling - Kusnacht - located on Lake Zurich. However, Kussnacht am Rigi is a little village on the northern tip of a small finger of Lake Lucerne. This is a charming town with some colorful medieval buildings. Since there is ferry service from Lucerne, Kussnacht is popular for a day's excursion or an overnight stay.

LUGANO

Lugano is an appealing medieval town hugging the northern shore of Lake Lugano. While in Lugano, there are several "musts". First, you will love exploring the old city. This is not only *best* done by walking, but actually *must* be done on foot since many of the streets are closed to cars. Be sure to visit the cathedral of St. Lawrence (San Lorenzo) which is famous for its elegant renaissance facade and lovely fresco decoration. Also, Lugano has one of the very finest art museums in Switzerland located in the suburbs on the lake at Castagnola. This museum, *VILLA FAVORITA*, is a villa exquisitely set on the lake and contains works of art from the middle ages to the nineteenth century. Here you will find such treasures as paintings by Rubens, Van Dyck, Raphael, and Titian. Try to plan time in Lugano to visit this special museum, but double check the days and times open since it is a private museum and is frequently closed. Another "must" for Lugano is to take advantage of the steamers which ply the lake from its dock. You can stretch your boat ride out to an all day excursion or squeeze it into a couple of hours. My recommendation would be to go to Morcote which is a charming little lake side town rising from the shores of the lake. If possible, allow time enough in Morcote to have lunch in the gay little over water cafe in front of the Ticino Hotel. If you feel industrious, you can climb up the steep back alleys rising from the lakefront which will bring you to the church of Santa Maria Del Sasso which contains some outstanding sixteenth century frescoes. Also in Morcote is a delightful private park. Here you will find beautiful plants gorgeously displayed in a lakeside garden. The gardens are only a few minutes walk from the Ticino Hotel but are open to the public only at brief times. Another fun boat trip from

Lugano is to Gandria, another village clinging to the lakeside filled with flowers and surrounded by vineyards. Both Gandria and Morcote are photographers' dreams. Another boat trip out of Lugano would be to the small town of Castagnola. If possible, plan to go when you can visit the Villa Favorita mentioned above as such a special museum. But even if the museum is closed, this is a fun stop because there is a foot path which runs along the lake front for about a mile to the next little town. Along this path, there are lovely views of the lake and several places such as Fischer's See Hotel where you can stop for lunch overlooking the waterfront.

LUCERNE

There is not a wealth of tourist attractions in Lucerne. The attraction is the city itself. Nor will you feel you have "discovered" Lucerne. Frankly, it is brimming with tourists. However, you will certainly understand why as you wander the charming little streets filled with colorful shops; stroll the river promenade stopping for a snack in one of the quaint cafes set out on the banks of the Reuss River; criss-cross back and forth from one side of the river to the other enjoying the pleasure of savoring the romantic character of each bridge; meander along the shore of Lake Lucerne stopping to watch the ferries loaded with merry passengers; board one of the steamers for a lazy journey around the lake. Yes, tourists have "found" Lucerne, but it is so lovely, I do not think you will mind sharing it with others.

Located in Lucerne is the *MUSEUM OF TRANSPORT AND COMMUNICATIONS*, one of the finest museums in Switzerland. This display follows the development of all forms of transportation and communication up to the astronauts. If traveling with children, they will especially be enthralled with this wonderful museum.

On a sunny day, there is an outing from Lucerne to the highest mountain peak in the area, *MOUNT PILATUS*. The most enjoyable route for this excursion is to take the lake steamer to the town of Alpnachstad and then the electric cog railway up to the top of the mountain. From the top of the rail terminal it is only about a ten minute walk to the peak of the mountain where there is a spectacular panorama.

Another excursion from Lucerne is to the town of *EINSIEDELN* to see the home of the famous *"BLACK MADONNA"*. The monastery of Einsiedeln was founded by Meinrad, a Benedictine monk, who built a small chapel for the Black Madonna which had been given to him by Zurich priests. Meinrad was later murdered by some men who mistakenly thought he had hidden treasures. Later the Monastery of Einsiedeln was built over Meinrad's grave and a chapel erected to house the Black Madonna. This site has become a pilgrimage, not only for Catholics, but for tourists who are attracted to the Einsiedeln Abbey which is an excellent example of Baroque architecture.

MURTEN

Murten is a sensational walled medieval village nestled on the banks of Lake Murten - only a short distance from Berne or Neuchatel. You enter Murten through a gate in one of the medieval walls which completely surround this fairy tale village. In summer the town is ablaze with color. Flower boxes are everywhere. Brightly painted fountains accent the small squares. The entire effect is one of festivity. Before exploring the town you might want to first climb the staircase to the ramparts and walk the walls for a bird's eye view of what you are going to see. Murten is like an outdoor museum. Strolling through the town you can study many of the fifteenth century buildings and the walls which date from the twelfth century. There is a castle at the western end of town built by Peter of Savoy in the thirteenth century. As you walk through the village watch for the Town Hall, the French Church, the German Church, the Berne Gate (which has one of the oldest clock towers in Switzerland) , and the Historical Museum which displays weapons, banners, and uniforms from the Burgundian battles.

REGENSBERG

Regensberg is very, very special. It is actually almost a miracle. Here only a few miles north of Zurich, and about twenty minutes from the Zurich Airport, is a perfectly preserved medieval village "icing" the knoll of a small hill charmingly laced with vineyards. An even greater miracle is that in this town is one of the most exquisite little inns in Switzerland, The Rote Rose. The Rote Rose is owned by the world famous rose artist, Lotte Gunthart and is managed by her delightful daughter, Christa Schafer. Regensberg is perfect for your arrival into Zurich or a wonderful choice for few days to relax before departing from the Zurich Airport.

REICHENBACH

Reichenbach, a small town located in the Kandertal Valley, makes a convenient base for sightseeing or hiking. In additional to the many hiking trails branching out from Reichenbach, you are centrally located for many excursions such as the the *JUNGFRAU, THUN, INTERLAKEN, KANDERSTEG, BLAUSEE, and LAKE OESCHINEN.*

SAAS-FEE

Saas-Fee is located at the end of a little valley which branches off from the road to the famous resort of Zermatt. However, whereas Zermatt is built on the floor of the valley, Saas-Fee is situated on a small terrace high above the valley floor. There are similarities though between the two towns. Both are closed to automobile traffic, both are excellent ski areas, both have beautifully marked walking trails, and both try to preserve the Alpine chalet architecture. Zermatt is more of the "Jet-Set" resort with large hotels, expensive shops, gourmet restaurants, and "night life". Saas-Fee has the reputation of being more of a family resort.

SANTA MARIA

Santa Maria is a small hamlet intersected by the road through the beautiful Mustair Valley. There are many lovely old Grison style buildings in the town and a very attractive church. Also, nearby is the Swiss National Park which is an oasis for wild life and vegetation. The park is very popular with the Swiss who come here frequently to hike the beautifully marked trails with their families.

SCHAFFHAUSEN

Schaffhausen is a delightful medieval city which grew up along the banks of the Rhine River just above the point where the Rhine Falls, *Rheinfall*, interrupted the passage of the boats which plied the river. Because the boats could not continue beyond this point, the cargo had to be carried around the falls and therefore the city of Schaffhausen grew up to accommodate the trade. There are many very colorful houses - really architectural "gems" within Schaffhausen - many with the famous "oriel" windows adding colorful detail. There are also several fountains, old towers, and of course, a castle above the city on a knoll of a hill. While in Schaffhausen you will certainly want to make the very short excursion to see the Rheinfall. Where the cascading falls reach the bottom of the river there is a dock where you can take a boat right out to the bottom of the falls. Another excursion from Schaffhausen is to the walled town of Stein am Rhein. This little town is to the east of Schaffhausen and as the name implies also built along the Rhein. Stein am Rhein is packed with tourists during the summer season, but it is one of the most photogenic towns in Switzerland. After entering the main gates of the little town you find yourself in a fairy tale village with each building almost totally covered with fanciful paintings. The town is very small so it won't take long to "do" the town but it is certainly worth a visit.

SILS-BASELGIA

Just a few miles south of the famous resort of St. Moritz is the little town of Sils-Baselgia located on a thread of land which connects the two tiny lakes of Silvaplana and Silser. Sils area is a wonderful headquarters for cross country skiing in the winter and in the summer hiking, boating, fishing, sail surfing, and swimming.

SILVAPLANA

Silvaplana is a small town about four miles south of St. Moritz. There is much more of the small mountain village feeling at Silvaplana than its next door neighbor, but this is still a bustling summer and winter resort.

SOGLIO

The mountain setting of the little town of Soglio is one of the most dramatically beautiful in all of Switzerland. In fact Mr Isler, who manages the Swiss National Tourist Office in San Francisco, told me that a travel writer had seen pictures of Soglio and just couldn't believe they were real and went himself to confirm that this perfect village existed. Frankly, this is how I also found Soglio. I had seen a drawing of the town in a travel guide and immediately I knew I had to see it myself. The town of Soglio is perched on a ledge high above the beautiful Bregaglia Valley. The town is tiny with just a few little streets lined with wonderful old houses with an Italian feeling. The church is perfect, setting off the picture book village with its high spire soaring into the sky. The village looks across the valley to some of the most impressive mountain peaks in Switzerland.

Soglio is not only a picturesque stopover, but in addition it is a wonderful center for walking. There are beautiful paths leading out from Soglio which run along the ledge of the mountain. Chestnut trees line some of the beautiful trails and although you are high above the valley the walking is easy.

SOLOTHURN

The town of Solothurn, one of the oldest Roman settlements in Switzerland, is a completely walled medieval city built along the shore of the Aare River. A modern industrial city has grown up around Solothurn, but once you cross through the gate, like magic you are transported back hundreds of years. This pretty medieval town has remained unspoiled. You are greeted by colorfully painted fountains, charming little squares, beautifully preserved buildings, the famous St. Ursen Cathedral, wrought iron signs, and houses with brightly painted shutters.

VERBIER

Verbier has a spectacular setting on a high mountain plateau overlooking the valley to the glorious Mont Blanc Mountain range. Although the village of Verbier has the air of a newly created modern mountain town, there are still many of the older wooden chalets around to remind you that before the skiers came to this sunny mountain slope it was an originally a typical Valais Village.

WENGEN

Part of the charm of Wengen is that it can only be reached by train. You can leave your car in the parking lot at the Lauterbrunnen station and take the train for the spectacular twenty minute ride up the mountain. As the train pulls up the mountain you catch glimpses through the lacey trees of the magnificent valley below enclosed by steep walls decorated with gushing water falls. Wengen has one of the most glorious sites in the world. It is located on a mountain plateau overlooking the Lauterbrunnen Valley whose walls are laced with cascading water falls and beyond to the awe inspiring mountains. This is a center for outdoor enthusiasts and sportsmen. From all over the world tourists come to soak up spectacular mountain beauty. Summer is my favorite time of year in Wengen when the marvelous walking paths beckon you to wander. Along these trails there are new vistas at every turn, each more beautiful than the last. If walking is too gentle for your spirit, there are climbs you can take into the Bernese Oberland. If you are going to do some serious climbing you should hire a local guide to accompany you. In addition to being a mecca for the mountain enthusiast, Wengen also is an excellent base for the excursion to the Jungfrau. *PLEASE REFER TO JUNGFRAU SIGHTSEEING.*

ZERMATT

Cars are not allowed in Zermatt. However this is no problem as there are car parks at each of the towns as you approach Zermatt. I would suggest leaving your car at Tasch which is the last town prior to your arrival. From here it is only a few minutes train ride in to Zermatt. As you arrive at the station you will notice many horse drawn carriages awaiting your train. In winter, these become horse drawn sleighs. In the past few years, little electric golf-type carts have gradually replaced some of the horse drawn carriages.

Zermatt is not the sleepy little mountain village of yesterday! In fact, it is difficult to uncover the remnants of the "Old Zermatt" - the weathered wooden chalets weighted beneath heavy slate roofs. True, they are still there hidden on little side alleys and dotted in the mountain meadows, but as you wander Zermatt you are bombarded with the effects of the growth of tourism: shopping arcades stretching out behind old store fronts, hotels expanding, new condominiums springing up in the meadows, tourists packing the streets. I know this sounds awful. It isn't. Zermatt is still one of my favorite places in Switzerland. Some things never change. The Matterhorn, rising in majestic splendor as a backdrop to the village, is still one of the most dramatic sights in the world. And, as you leave the center of Zermatt, within a few minutes you are again in the "Zermatt of Old" with gigantic mountain peaks piercing the sky. It is so beautiful that it is frustrating - each path is beckoning "try me"! You want to go every direction at once.

The great influx of tourists definitely has advantages too. Fun little shops filled with tempting wares line the streets. Cozy restaurants make each meal decision a dilemma. New hotels have opened giving the traveler a great selection of accommodations. The pride of making Zermatt worthy of its reputation has stimulated competition among the hoteliers and shopkeepers - each appears to strive to make his flower box more gorgeous than his neighbor's resulting in a profusion of color. The popularity of Zermatt has also merited a fascinating network of trails lacing the mountains. These are used in summer for walking and in winter for skiing. A small train runs up to the Gornergrat station which is located on a rocky ridge overlooking the town of Zermatt and beyond to the Matterhorn. There are also cable cars and chair lifts rising like a spider web around Zermatt. There is an incredible choice for the tourist. When hiking, it is possible to either choose beautifully marked trails drifting out from the village core, or to take one of the chairs lifts or trams or train up the mountain, from which point you can walk all or part way down. The number of tourists also justifies numerous small cafes scattered along the trails. It is truly a "gentleman's" way to hike when you can stop along the route at a little outdoor restaurant for a glass of wine. Zermatt is truly "the Switzerland" of our childhood books and a trip to Switzerland is never quite complete without a visit to see the Matterhorn.

ZURICH

In Zurich there is much to see and do. On a warm day I suggest taking an excursion on one of the steamers which ply the lovely Lake Zurich. There is a schedule posted at each of the piers stating where the boats go and when they depart. During the summer there is frequent service and a wide selection to suit your mood and your time frame.

Zurich is also a great city for just meandering through the medieval section with its maze of tiny twisting streets, colorful squares, charming little shops, and tempting cafes. It is fun to walk down the promenade by the Limmat river to the lake front and cross over the Quailbrucke (bridge) and return by the opposite bank. When weary, cross back over one of the bridges which span the river to complete your "circle."

For those of you who like museums, the *SWISS NATIONAL MUSEUM* has a display depicting Swiss civilization from prehistoric times to modern day. Zurich's *FINE ARTS MUSEUM* is well worth a visit. Of special interest here are some of the paintings of Ferdinand Hodler, one of the finest Swiss artists of the early twentieth century. Also on display are some of the paintings of my favorite Swiss artist, Anker, whose delightful paintings capture the warmth of family and home with simplicity and humor.

For the cathedral buffs, there is the impressive *GROSSMUNSTER* whose construction dates back to the eleventh century. This is a very impressive cathedral dominating Zurich with its two-domed towers. To add to the romance of this cathedral is the story that it was built on a site originally occupied by a church built by Charlemagne!

Itineraries

Swiss Highlights

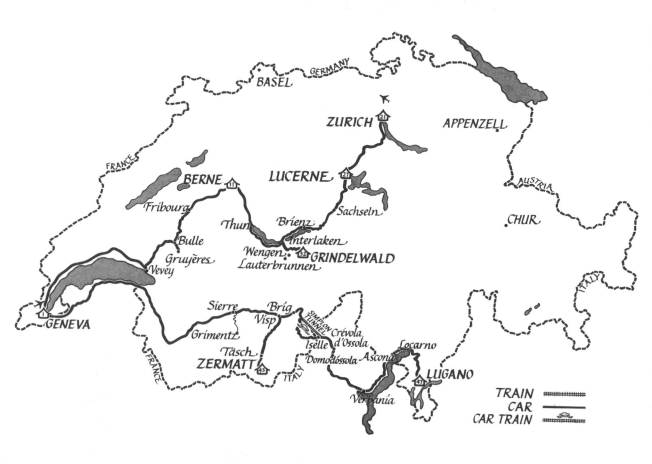

TRAIN
CAR
CAR TRAIN

FOR THE TRAVELER who wants to see the highlights of Switzerland including the the "picture book perfect" destinations repeatedly seen on post cards and read about in books, this is an ideal itinerary. The following path will lead you through some of the most scenic areas of Switzerland and introduce you to a wonderful variety of famous cities, charming villages, beautiful lakes, lush valleys, and splendid mountains. Although you will not be wandering into the tiny hamlets and back roads suggested in some of following routes, this tour is definitely *not* a compromise! The towns and destinations included are famous because they are outstanding. They deserve the accolades of enthusiasm. They deserve the loyalty of tourists returning year after year to enjoy their spectacular beauty.

If you only have a few days you can take segments of this itinerary. As an example, you could take only the Zurich to Geneva portion. If you have already, on previous holidays, enjoyed Zurich, Lucerne, and Interlaken (one of the most famous trios) you could begin this itinerary in Geneva and end it in the Swiss-Italian Lake District. If your time is extremely limited, you could very easily journey from Zurich to Geneva in one day - even enjoying some sightseeing along the way. I hope this itinerary will provide a framework to piece together your own *Custom Highlights Tour*.

If your arrival is by plane, the Zurich Airport is an excellent introduction to marvelous Swiss efficiency. As in all countries, you must identify and collect your luggage, but once that task is accomplished, the Swiss have managed to eliminate most of the hassle and have conscientiously made life as simple as possible for the traveler. There is no need to bother with porters or suffer the burden of economizing by dragging your bags along at your side, as there are usually an ample number of luggage carts neatly lined up ready for your free use. After loading your baggage on a cart, you do not have to go through any customs inspection of your luggage unless you have something to declare. Once through the baggage area, everything is well marked. If you need to make a hotel reservation, there is a desk set up for this purpose. If you want a car rental, this too is well marked. If you want to take the train into either Zurich or directly to many of the other towns in Switzerland, the train station or *bahnhof*, is located on the lower level. There is also an information booth for the train where you can ask directions and buy tickets directly to the left as you exit customs. There is a counter where you can check your baggage to any train or bus station in Switzerland. There are also many shops, a post office, banks, etc. all efficiently set up and identified. When I first came out of Customs with the luggage cart seeking the train station, I was concerned as the arrows pointed down the escalator. Again, no problem. The Swiss have thought of everything. There are directions on each luggage cart showing how to take it on the escalator with you. You can take your cart all the way to the train or, if renting a car, directly to your car.

Taking the train into Zurich is really the quickest and most efficient means of transportation unless you have several persons in your party. In this case a cab might prove preferable.

For your first night in Switzerland I recommend a favorite in Zurich. The *ZUM STORCHEN* is not country inn. It is a modern hotel with all the amenities a large city hotel has to offer, but underneath the modern improvements still emerges the charm of one of the oldest hotels in Switzerland. It has a wonderful location rising directly from the waters of the Limmat River a short distance before it flows into Lake Zurich.

HOTEL ZUM STORCHEN

Even if you are planning your holiday as a driving vacation, I would suggest refraining from picking up your car until after you leave Lucerne. The roads are very congested between Zurich and Lucerne and at this time, there are no freeways. Within both cities, there is no need for a car. In fact, a car becomes somewhat of a nuisance. Walking is one of the major attractions of both cities. Therefore, in this particular itinerary, I suggest you take the train from Zurich to Lucerne. There are trains constantly plying back and forth between the two, it is a most pleasant journey, taking just about an hour.

WILDEN MANN HOTEL

In Lucerne, the *WILDEN MANN* is the perfect inn within a city. Rarely do you find a hotel, except in the countryside, that retains such a cozy, intimate feeling. The owner, Mr. Furler and his wife personally oversee every tiny aspect of this charming, antique filled hotel located in the heart of the medieval section of Lucerne and their dedication shows in every detail.

DESTINATION   III :   GRINDELWALD   *HOTEL FIESCHERBLICK*

Enroute for Grindelwald head south from Lucerne toward Hergswil. Near Stansstad follow the highway south toward Brienz, passing the town of Sachseln located on Lake Sarner about midway to Brienz. At the center of Sachseln is achurch which served as a very important pilgrimage of Swiss Catholics. Within the nave are the remains of St. Nicholas of Flue who is not only a religious, but also a patriotic hero of the Swiss. St. Nicholas gained fame in the fifteenth century when he is credited with keeping peace within Switzerland and furthering the growth of the confederation. A peasant, he had a reputation as a fair and peace-loving man. When there was danger that some of the Cantons might go to war over disagreements, the parish priests went to consult brother Nicholas and through his wisdom, a compromise was worked out and instead of a battle, Solothurn and Fribourg joined the confederation in 1481. After leaving Sachseln, pass through the little towns of Giswil, Daiserbuhl, and Lungern before going over the Brunig Pass. The road leads downward from the Brunig Pass to the town of Brienz located at the east end of Lake Brienz. The town of Brienz is beautifully situated on the lake and is a very popular summer resort. Brienz is also one of the centers for woodcarving in Switzerland. The ride along the north side of Lake Brienz is beautiful with lovely views of the lake as you pass through the little towns of Oberried and Niederried and Ringgenberg before arriving at Interlaken.

Interlaken, the name means "between lakes", is situated on a neck of land joining Brienz Lake with Thun Lake. The location is fabulous with two gorgeous lakes stretching out on each side of the town plus excellent views of the Jungfrau Mountain. Understandably the town has been a center of tourism for years. There are many large Victorian-style hotels, inviting shops and cafes lining the streets. Although a bit touristy one can never dispute the spectacular location nor deny that it is a convenient stopover for the circle trip by rail to see the Jungfrau.

However, the suggested alternative to staying in Interlaken is to journey on and head instead to where the mountains are right at your fingertips. Leaving Interlaken in the direction of Lauterbrunnen, it is only a short drive until the road splits. At the junction head left along a gorgeous road as you climb upwards toward the little town of Grindelwald.

HOTEL FIESCHERBLICK

Grindelwald is the closest mountain village to which you can drive when visiting the Jungfrau. The setting of this glacier village is spectacular with views of three giant mountain peaks, the Eiger, the Mettenberg, and the Wetterhorn. Grindelwald serves as a perfect gateway for the train ride up to the Jungfrau and is also a haven for hikers and climbers.

Grindelwald has a number of fancy and deluxe hotels but there is a special attraction for and quality to the *FIESCHERBLICK HOTEL*. The accommodations are unpretentious and basic in decor but, although simple, many rooms enjoy mountain views. The personalized and home-spun atmosphere is inviting and seems so appropriate in a town that is dwarfed by the magnificence of the surrounding peaks. A small hotel owned by the Brawand-Hauser family, the Fiescherblick is located across the street from the small church as you drive through the village. The hotel actually used to be the family dwelling and the artistically displayed antique farm implements are from the family farm. There is a dining room on the first floor and when the weather is suitable, tables are set out in front of the hotel and also on a raised patio.

Allow two days for Grindelwald for you will need most of one day for the Jungfrau circuit. Allow more days if you also want to enjoy the beauty of the mountains. This is an ideal spot for strenuous mountain climbing or leisurely sightseeing.

DESTINATION   IV :   BERNE   *BELLEVUE PALACE HOTEL*

From Grindelwald return to Interlaken and then take the highway marked to Thun. If you have allocated the whole day to sightseeing, a stop at Thun, located at the west end of Thun Lake, would prove the ideal spot for lunch. Thun is a picturesque medieval village with a castle crowning the hillside. Now a museum the castle is open to the public. From the castle turrets is a beautiful panorama of Thun, the lake and mountains beyond. Getting to the castle is fun because the pathway from the village to the castle is via a covered staircase.

Leaving Thun, stay on the expressway to Berne. It is only a short drive and the faster road will afford more time for sightseeing in Berne.

Another of the beautifully preserved medieval towns, Berne is nestled in a loop of the Aare River at a point where the river banks fall steeply to the river below. To further enhance the setting, the Alps rise in the background. The setting alone would make Berne worth a stop, but the town has much to offer in addition to its picturesque location. A storybook town with lots of character and things to see, Berne dates to the beginning of the thirteenth century.

BELLEVUE PALACE

Situated at the edge of the intriguing old sector of the city is the elegant *BELLEVUE PALACE HOTEL*. With such an excellent location it is an ideal base to explore Berne on foot. From the Bellevue Palace you can walk to most of the tourist attractions or wander the arcaded sidewalks. The whole town seems to have a festive air from its comical fountains to its jolly clock tower.

DESTINATION   V :   GENEVA   *LE RICHEMOND*

Leaving Berne, it is just a short drive south to the town of Fribourg, located on the banks of the Sarine River. It is a beautifully preserved medieval city with its town hall, cathedral of St. Nicholas, clock tower, and the church of Notre-Dame. Since you have just been in Berne, which is even more colorful than Fribourg, you might want to bypass this city and instead allocate your precious sightseeing time to a complete change of pace, the charming town of Gruyeres.

Gruyeres is located only a few miles off the freeway running south from Berne. After leaving Fribourg, you soon see signs to Bulle and Gruyeres. At that point, you will need to leave the freeway. After passing through the town of Bulle you will soon spot Gruyeres crowning the top of a small hill. This village is actually one main street of beautifully preserved buildings. At the end of the street is a castle, open to the public daily during summer. Gruyeres is such a wonderful little town that it is considered a national monument and its architecture is protected by the government. Cars cannot be driven into the town, but parking is provided on the road leading up the hill to the village. The town attracts so many tourists that its unique appeal during the tourist season is marred somewhat by mobs of people. However, it is such a picturesque spot with such beautiful views of green meadows and mountains that it is certainly worth the detour. It is in the center of a dairy area and the cheese and creams are marvelous. Stop for a famous Gruyeres quiche or if in season, fresh berries and cream...fantastic.

Leaving Gruyeres, return again to the highway and continue south toward Vevey. From Vevey, take the freeway west toward Geneva. An alternative to the freeway would be to travel the lakeside road. Enroute there are many charming little waterfront towns, however the traffic is very congested and the vistas are actually more magnificent from the freeway. From its vantage point, you see across the lake to the mountains beyond.

Geneva is a lovely city graced by a French influence. Geneva is frequently thought of as a "new" city - a city of banking and commerce, an international city housing the Place Des Nations, a city of beautiful shops, a city of museums and culture, an industrial city. It also has one of the most attractive old towns in Switzerland. On the south side of the Rhone River the hills rise steeply and twist

LE RICHEMOND

and turn in a maze full of little shops, fountains, flowers, and charming buildings. This area is crowned by St. Peter's Cathedral which dominates the old town.

Geneva is also known for the majestic queens which nestle on the right side of the lake and *LE RICHEMOND* is a favorite of these formal lakeside hotels.

DESTINATION   VI :   ZERMATT   *HOTEL JULEN*

Leaving Geneva you can circle the lake either by the north shore or the south shore. The road to the south is slower because it takes you through all the small villages, but two-thirds of the route exposes you to the flavor of France. The road to the north of Lake Geneva has two choices, and depending on time you may choose either a fast express way or the small road which meanders through the little towns. At the east end of Lake Geneva the Rhone River makes its way down a flat valley. The mountains rise steeply from the edge of the valley and on the lower hills are clustered the vineyards which make the Rhone Valley so famous. The section of the Rhone Valley when traveling from Lake Geneva to the Zermatt turnoff is beautiful, but not the pristine beauty found so much in the other Swiss valleys. It passes through many industrial areas. However, there are countless side valleys and small passes to explore running off the Rhone Valley into the mountains both to the north and to the south. All of these are small twisting roads geared to the young at heart, well worth a detour if you have the time. A favorite is a pass climbing up to the tiny village of Grimentz. The turnoff for Grimentz is near the city of Sierre. At Sierre, watch carefully for signs for the road which runs to the south of the highway.

Grimentz is a delightful little village. Like so many of the other towns which retain much of their original charm, the government protects the architectural standards. This is a town of small, wooden Valais-style homes, darkened almost black with age. The houses usually have a slate roof and are set upon stone pillars. It is hard to believe that the Grimentz of old could ever be as lovely as it is today for each resident seems to vie with his neighbor for the most gorgeous displays of brilliant red geraniums. The effect is glorious with the brilliant blue sky (with a little luck!) , snow-capped mountains, green pastures, and darkened wooden houses with flower boxes exploding in color.

As the road is physically demanding it is suggested not to undertake this side trip in the winter, but in the summer if the day is clear, and if you do not mind a rather precarious road, then Grimentz would be a very worthwhile detour. Try to time it so that you arrive at the lunch hour and so can enjoy a local cheese fondue on the outdoor patio of the De Moiry Hotel. From here, you can savor your lunch together with an incredibly lovely view of the valley below and the mountain wall facing you.

If you have taken the side-trip to Grimentz, return to the freeway, continue in the same direction as before and take the turnoff for Zermatt as you near Visp. The only choice you have along the way is where the road splits and the left branch of the road leads to Saas-Fee and the right branch leads to Zermatt. You cannot drive into Zermatt as no cars are allowed within the city limits. However, this is no problem as there are car parks at each of the small towns on the approach to Zermatt. Tasch is the last town prior to Zermatt and here you can leave your car and take the train into Zermatt. This is only a few minutes ride. Upon arrival at the Zermatt train station, you will notice many horse drawn carriages. In winter, these convert to horse drawn sleighs. In the past few years, little electric golf-type carts have gradually replaced some of the horses and sleds. Most of the major hotels will send their "carriage" to meet the incoming train. Each hotel has their name on the cart or carriage or the porter's cap. If for some reason the porter is not there, you will find many electric taxis also available to take you to your hotel.

HOTEL JULEN

The *HOTEL JULEN* is located just beyond Zermatt's city center so you feel you are somewhat out of the bustle of the tourist rush. The hotel has a wonderful "olde worlde charm" with a cozy fireplace in the reception hall, antiques artfully placed throughout, a charming restaurant and a cheerful little patio in the rear garden. If you are very lucky, you might even be able to have one of the bedrooms from which you can watch the various moods of the majestic Matterhorn.

Zermatt is truly "the Switzerland" of our childhood books and a trip to Switzerland is never quite complete without a visit to see the Matterhorn.

It is a long day from Zermatt to the Swiss-Italian Lake District. The journey involves travel both by car and train. In order to coordinate schedules and allow for enough time, an early departure is suggested. First you need to return by train from Zermatt to Tasch, pick up your car at Tasch and drive to the town of Brig. (This is about an hour's drive.)

If you want to include a little sightseeing prior to your journey from Brig, I would recommend stopping to visit Stockalperschloss which is one of the most interesting castles in Switzerland. It was built by a very wealthy merchant, Kaspar Jodok Stockalper Von Thurm in the seventeenth century. This castle was the largest private residence in Switzerland and is now open to the public May to October from 9 AM to 11 AM and from 2 PM to 5 PM. The castle is closed on Mondays. There are frequently guided tours which take about forty-five minutes.

The portion of your journey by train begins at Brig. From here you travel over the mountains and across the border into Italy. You do not abandon your car but rather reserve space for it on the train as well. Try to time you arrival at about half past the hour because the train departs on the hour from Brig. When you arrive into Brig, follow the signs for the train station. At the train station, purchase the ticket which permits you to take your car on the train from Brig through the Simplon Tunnel then follow the signs to where you put your car onto the train. (Putting your car on the train to go over a special pass or through a tunnel is quite common in Switzerland and the sign is always the same - a train car with an automobile sitting on it.) The signs will direct you to the road leading to the left of the station which circles over the train tracks and then veers to the right and ends up at the track on the opposite side of the station. At this point, there are signs showing you which lane to get into for the train. The train will arrive about ten minutes before the hour and the sides of the train are let down level with the street and you drive on. The train you require is the one going to Iselle. This is at the opposite end of the Simplon Tunnel and is the Italian town at which you will be directed to drive your car off the train. Keep your ticket because it is at this point where you turn it in as proof of payment.

Please consider, however, if you have any problem with claustrophobia, you might not like the train ride and can, of course, always take the option of driving the twisting Simplon Pass. But if you don't mind dark spaces, the train ride is quite a thrill. Walt Disney would have had trouble devising a more dramatic tunnel. The Simplon Tunnel is one of the longest in the world It is twelve miles long and you enter the tunnel as soon as the train leaves Brig. The ride inside your car is in total darkness and swings back and forth for about twenty minutes. It is quite an adventure and saves probably an hours driving time.

HOTEL TICINO

When you descend from the train in Iselle, you continue south a short distance first to the town of Crevoladossola, and a few minutes further on, Domodossola. There are signs at Crevoladossola to direct you left along a road to Locarno. This is a "short cut" to the Swiss Italian lakes. It is truly a spectacular drive following a river gorge. But frankly, it is a very narrow road and a bit treacherous. I would recommend sticking to the main highway and heading south toward Verbania and then following Lake Maggiore north toward Locarno. Before reaching Locarno is the little town of Ascona nestled at the northern end of the lake. This would be a good place to sit and have lunch or a cup of coffee at one of the many street side cafes which overlook the lake. My favorite is the cafe in front of the dear Tamaro Hotel. After a break for a snack and perhaps a little shopping spree in one of the ancient little streets branching out behind the lake front, look for the freeway signs to speed up your journey from Ascona to Lugano.

I must warn you that Lugano is a complicated city in which to find your way to the heart of the old section. First be sure to have a good map and next you will need patience! Even though you can pin point on the map where you want to go, it is not easy. You might have to make several loops about the old town on the main one-way streets until you finally succeed in squeezing your way into the old section. Take heart, it is worth the effort. Although from the outskirts Lugano looks like an unattractive large metropolis, once you are in the heart of the city you discover the Lugano of old.

Tucked away in this atmospheric section of Lugano is the delightful *TICINO HOTEL*. Fronting a small square, the Piazza Cioccaro, the Ticino is tiny but full of charm. To the left of the hotel's entrance is a small grocery shop with its wares so colorfully displayed it seems more like a stage setting. To the right of the reception area is a small dining room - intimate and attractive. To the rear of the reception desk are stairs leading up to the bedrooms. The rooms themselves are quite simple but attractive. On the upper levels of the hotel are various small cozy corners for reading or lounging. Antiques accent all the little nooks and crannies. Green plants complete the picture of a hotel done with style and taste.

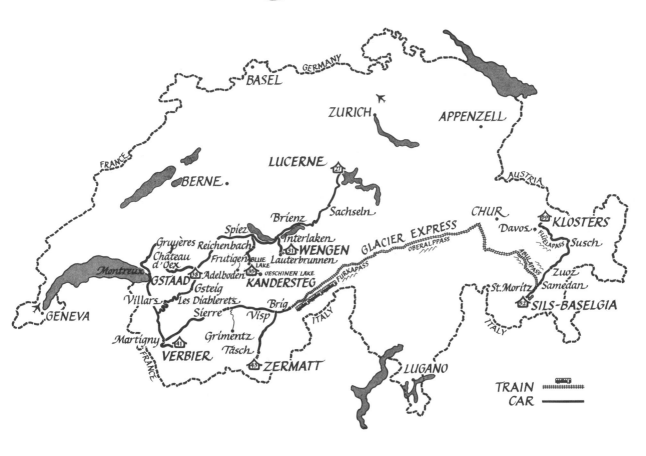

Mountain Adventures

THIS ITINERARY IS FOR the true mountain lover, for the traveler whose year will be happier for the memory of a perfect sunset over the mountain tops, whose problems will shrink into perspective as the mind wanders back to wonderful meadows full of flowers extending to snow capped mountains, whose tensions will fade as the soul recalls the stroll up a gorgeous mountain path.

To enjoy this itinerary, you need not be an Olympic champion, just enjoy being outside. You will be right in style as long as you have the one common denominator - love of the mountains. Of course if you are a mountain climber, the beckoning of the Matterhorn will probably be overwhelming and I wish for you a perfect few days to obtain your desire. If you enjoy skiing then of course the slopes of Gstaad will be irresistible. However, if you simply like to stroll the tiny pathways and if your greatest exertion will probably be to stoop to pick a wild flower, you too will be right at home..

The mountain resorts of Switzerland team with a varied array of Swiss and other Europeans enjoying the mountain air and the walking trails. These holiday seekers for the most part are not your image of the disciplined, trim, serious athlete. The majority of fellow tourists are couples or families dressed in woollen sweaters, corduroy knickers, bright knee socks, sturdy walking shoes, and primitive walking sticks laughing and talking as they meander along the trails. Therefore feel most comfortable, no matter what your ability, to join this jovial, friendly group of "mountaineers".

If time is limited, you can enjoy the routing from Lucerne to Zermatt and end your trip there. Return to Lucerne or Zurich or Geneva or else head south to the Italian Lakes. However, if you can possibly extend your holiday, I would try the "Glacier Express" which is a private railroad connecting Zermatt and St. Moritz. This all day train ride over some of the most glorious mountain passes in the world is a highlight of any trip to Switzerland. Even if the visibility is zero, the journey on this little red train will still be fun. What a memorable experience to arrive at the train station in Zermatt by horse and sleigh (or horse and buggy in summer), climb onto the train, settle down in the clean bright compartment, enjoy a gourmet meal in the Victorian dining car, chat and laugh with fellow passengers, and arrive relaxed and happy in St. Moritz!

So, include all of these mountain villages, or if time is short, select the resorts which sound most suited to your personality. For Switzerland is blessed with the gift of alpine heights and lofty summits and to visit Switzerland is to enjoy her mountains. Don't go home without strolling some of the paths and soaking up some of the fabulous mountain vistas.

Because there are no international airports in the high mountain areas, this itinerary begins in one of Switzerland's most famous cities, Lucerne, a marvelous medieval town with a fairy tale setting on the lake with a beautiful mountain backdrop. Lucerne is connected by a direct train from the Zurich airport.

CHATEAU GUTSCH

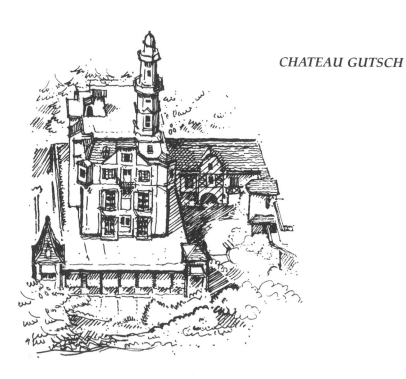

The *CHATEAU GUTSCH* seems a very appropriate hotel and a reservation here is an excellent beginning to your mountain adventure. Reached by a tramway the Chateau Gutsch is nestled on the hillside above Lucerne enjoying scenic vistas of the lake and city.

DESTINATION   II :   WENGEN   *REGINA HOTEL*

Today's destination is the town of Wengen in the famous Jungfrau area. The drive is easy and very beautiful. An early departure would be best enabling you to linger along the way. Head south from Lucerne toward Hergswil. Near Stansstad follow the highway south toward Brienz. On your way you will pass through the town of Sachseln located on Lake Sarner about midway to Brienz. This is a good stopping point if you want to include a coffee break with a little sightseeing. Sachseln is very famous for in the center of town is a beautiful church where St. Nicolas of Flue is buried. From Sachseln follow the highway to Brienz and then on to Interlaken. At Interlaken follow the signs south toward Lauterbrunnen. This is a lovely short drive but as far as you can go. At Lauterbrunnen you must park, leave your car and board a train for the last leg of your journey. As usual, the Swiss are extremely efficient and have organized a number of visual aids to simplify and outline the situation. The car park at Lauterbrunnen is well marked. Once your car is parked, follow the signs to the train station. The trains leave frequently. The ride up from Lauterbrunnen to Wengen is just spectacular! As the train climbs from the valley you look down as from an airplane to the Lauterbrunnen Valley. The journey is truly magnificent with steep cliff-like mountains rising steeply from the flat valley and towering water falls cascading down the sides, very reminiscent of the Yosemite Valley. It is only about a fifteen minute ride up to Wengen, but on a clear day, fifteen glorious minutes.

REGINA HOTEL

Wengen has one of the most glorious sites in the world located on a high mountain meadow overlooking the Lauterbrunnen Valley and beyond to the awe-inspiring mountains. This is a center for outdoor enthusiasts and sportsmen. From all over the world tourists come to soak up the mountain beauty. In winter ski sports are the dominant attraction. In the milder months the walking paths stretch out in every direction for the hiker offering a new vista at each turn, each more beautiful than the last. Leisured mountain viewing or gentle strolls are matched with strenuous mountain climbs of the Bernese Oberland for the more adventuresome of spirit. Mountain guides can be hired to give you advice and assistance. Remember to always consult a local guide if you are planning any serious climbing.

The *REGINA HOTEL* is a prime spot to stay in this very special town. When you arrive into Wengen by train the Regina usually has an electric cart at the station. If not, either call the hotel, or else leave your luggage at the station to be retrieved later and walk the short distance to the hotel. The Regina is perched on the hillside above and to the right of the train station. The hotel is reasonably priced so splurge and pay the additional for a room with one of the best views. The accommodations are bland but it is their very simplicity that sets off the unforgettable mountain splendor from your balcony. Jack Meyer, owner of the Regina is like a master of ceremonies and each day is an adventure as he orchestrates the management of the hotel down to the small details on the menu. An attentive host, Jack also takes on the responsibility for the happiness and social intermixing of his guests. After a few days at the Regina you will soon begin to feel like an honored guest and that the Regina is more like a house party than a hotel!

DESTINATION   III: KANDERSTEG   *ROYAL HOTEL BELLEVUE*

It will be difficult to leave the Jungfrau area but when you can wrench yourself away more splendor is awaiting you. A short drive back to Interlaken brings you again to the main highway circling the south side of Lake Thun. When you arrive at Interlaken turn left toward Speiz, then after about a twenty minute drive you will see the turn off for the Kandersteg Valley. Follow the signs towards Kandersteg. I highly recommend a stop about fifteen minutes after leaving Spiez at the small town of Reichenbach. There is a charming inn here called the Gasthof Baren with excellent food served in a beautiful country style dining room. The owner, Jacob Murner, is also the chef. Introduce yourself, Mr. Murner speaks beautiful English and is a perfect host. He can assist you in making a choice for lunch or dinner. After Reichenbach you will soon come to a fork in the road. Take the left branch toward Kandersteg.

At Kandersteg it will be easy to find the Royal Hotel Bellevue as the hotel is large for such a small town. The decor of the public rooms is very traditional and although the bedrooms might lack some country ambiance, the outside "decor" is unsurpassable! Request a room with a view of the mountains. Whereas the last town of Wengen was perched on a mountain shelf, Kandersteg is at the end of a valley. A marvelous meadow stretches out from behind the hotel extending to a majestic backdrop of mountains. There are lounge chairs on the lawn where you can sit and revel in the scenery.

ROYAL HOTEL BELLEVUE

From Kandersteg are an endless number of walks leading off to every point of the compass, each more tempting than the last. At the end of the village a chairlift rises from the valley to Lake Oeschinen where rugged cliffs jut dramatically out of the clear mountain lake. The lake lies below the terminal of the chairlift and is reached via a beautiful path through the mountain meadows. On a clear day this is a lovely outing, and for those rugged sports enthusiasts, the walk down can replace the chairlift ride on the return to Kandersteg.

Another outing from Kandersteg is to drive to the end of the other fork of the valley to the town of Adelboden. To do this, it is necessary to retrace the road a short distance to the town of Frutigen. At this town take the Engstigental Valley branching off to the left. This is a beautiful drive terminating at the town of Adelboden, a very attractive village with many old wooden farmhouses nestled on the hillside. Again, there is a fantastic backdrop of majestic mountain peaks. As you return to Kandersteg on the right hand side of the road are signs to the Blausee - Blue See. Park your car near the main road and walk along a wooded path through a forest of twisted, mysterious trees. You begin to wonder where in the world you are going when suddenly you come upon a tiny, gorgeous lake, a photographers's dream. The incredibly blue, clear lake, is set in the forest with a jagged alpine horizon. There are usually many people here as it is a favorite outing spot of the Swiss who like to come to eat lunch on the side of the lake in a little chalet type restaurant with tables set out on the terrace on mild days. This is also a popular stop for families with children who enjoy taking one of the boat rides or just circling the lake on the twisting little path following the shoreline amongst the gnarled forest. The effect is rather like a scene from Hansel and Gretel.

Kandersteg is also well known as the point from which the road ends and only the train continues on to the Rhone Valley. For those traveling by car in this direction the car can be put "piggy back" on the train for the ride through the mountains to Brig.

It is not a long journey from Kandersteg to Gstaad. Retrace the half a hour drive back toward Spiez and almost as soon as you reach the main road running along the shore of Lake Thun there is a branch off to the left which follows the lovely Simmental Valley. In less than an hour, you should reach the turnoff to Gstaad and then it is only another two miles to the town.

POST HOTEL ROSSLI

Stay at the *POSTHOTEL ROSSLI* located on a corner of the main street about midway through the town. This is another of the professionally managed, small, chalet-type hotels which has passed down from father to son. There are two excellent restaurants, one on each side of the main entrance hall. Both are done with a charming country motif. The present owner-manager is also a celebrated local mountaineer and has a reputation as an excellent winter ski guide.

In spite of the fact that it has an international reputation as a very chic ski resort catering to the wealthy jet set, Gstaad retains much of its old world, small town, charming simplicity. In fact, in summer you might awaken to the melody of cow bells as the herds are driven out to pasture. The setting of Gstaad is magnificent with the surrounding rugged mountain peaks. In summer the hiking or mountain climbing is excellent and in winter Gstaad offers one of the most famous network of trails for skiing in Switzerland.

DESTINATION V: VERBIER *HOTEL ROSALP*

One of the most scenic routes to Verbier is to continue on the road beyond Gstaad through the small village of Gsteig. Gsteig is situated at the end of the valley and from this point the road climbs sharply and twists and turns up the mountain via Les Diablerets and the famous ski resort of Villars and on down to the main highway of the Rhone Valley. This is a beautiful drive but probably closed in winter and in summer only recommended for those who enjoy mountain driving.

For the more feint of heart the easier driving route would be to return to the main highway and turn left toward Chateau a Oex and on to Gruyeres. On this alternate routing the Hostellerie St. Georges in Gruyeres would serve as an excellent stop for lunch. Sample some of the Gruyeres cheese served in the famous Swiss quiche and if berries are in season, they are a "must" smothered in the delicious Gruyeres cream, so thick it must practically be spooned onto the plate.

Just a few miles beyond Gruyeres the road joins the main freeway. At this point turn south toward Montreux. On the approach to Lake Geneva, the highway splits and you will need to go south through the Rhone Valley to the town of Martigny. Here turn right off the highway and follow the signs toward Verbier. The road winds through a small valley until suddenly just before Verbier it begins a series of hairpin turns and climbs sharply up the mountain side.

HOTEL ROSALP

Upon arrival in the famous mountain village of Verbier, secure reservations at the *HOTEL ROSALP*. The hotel's most outstanding claim to fame is Roland Pierroz, the owner, who is also the chef. Even other hoteliers, themselves gourmet chefs, proclaim Mr Pierroz to be one of the finest chefs in the country. Situated on the side of the mountain with glorious views of the Mont Blanc range, it is easy to enjoy the resort village of Verbier and feast on the skiing, hiking and dining! Although the village of Verbier has the air of a newly created modern mountain town, there are still many of the older wooden chalets around to remind you that before the skiers came to this mountain slope it was originally a typical Valais Village.

DESTINATION   VI : ZERMATT   *SEILER HOTEL MONTE ROSA*

From Verbier head back down the winding mountain road to Martigny and join the main highway traveling through the Rhone Valley. Follow the Rhone River Valley, noting the many famous vineyards clinging to the steep mountain sides. Unfortunately the scenery suffers a bit from the inevitable commercialization of the area, but if the day is clear and you are not in a rush, there are a number of little valleys branching off into box canyons to explore.

The most attractive side excursion would be to brave the exciting, but somewhat spine tingling, mountain road transecting the Val d'Anniviers and leading up to the town of Grimentz. The turnoff is near the town of Sierre. As you take the road up the valley, follow the left fork of the road when it splits and continue on to Grimentz, a beautifully preserved Valais Village high up on a mountain ridge. In summer it is a pretty sight with the dark weathered wooden Valais buildings set off in glorious splendor by window boxes filled with brilliant red geraniums. Enjoy fondue and the valley views from the deck of the Hotel Moiry before retracing your steps this time down the road!

As you approach Visp there will be signs directing you to the famous mountain retreat of Zermatt. As cars are not allowed in the town, it is necessary to park your car in Tasch and board the train for the remainder of your journey. Zermatt sits at the base of the Matterhorn, and almost as legendary as the familiar peak itself are the Seiler family hotels. It was from his doorstep on July 13,1865 that Alexander Seiler, owner of the *MONTE ROSA*, bid farewell to the historic group of seven that were the first to conquer the Matterhorn. To heed the advice of that first conqueror, Edward Whymper, who advertised the fame of the Monte Rosa by consistently responding to the the inquiry, *What is the best hotel in Zermatt?*, or *Where shall we go?*, with *GO TO THE MONTE ROSA - GO TO SEILER'S!*...and so shall you!

SEILER HOTEL MONTE ROSA

To reach the next mountain highlight destination you can certainly drive. However a rather unique experience would be to take the Glacier Express. This is a train on a private railroad running from Zermatt via Brig, continuing east through the end of the Rhone Valley, through the Furka Pass Tunnel, over the Oberalppass and the Albulapass, and into St. Moritz. The train is a delightful way to traverse this spectacular, awe inspiring route filled with high mountain passes.

If you do choose to take the train it will take a little planning. Based on research at the time of publication the following details were correct, but naturally may have changed in the meantime.

First, concerning the car rental, Hertz is the only major car rental company that allows you to to drop off your car in Brig. You can board the Glacier Express in Zermatt, but there are no rental companies there since cars are not allowed into Zermatt. Therefore, make prior arrangements to return your rental car to Brig and allow ample time to find the Hertz outlet and to complete the paperwork and still have time to catch the train. Upon arrival in Brig, to avoid the hassle of carrying luggage stop first at the station to leave your bags and then return the car rental. The Hertz office is located a few blocks behind the train station. Allow at least an hour and a half to avoid any possible delay. You do not want to miss the Glacier Express which will leave Brig exactly on schedule. At the time of this writing the train departs Brig at 11:44 AM arriving St Moritz at 5:52 PM. Very important however, since the timing is so important and schedules do change, is to please CONFIRM the schedule.

Also necessary to preplan is a car rental "at the other end". Several car rental companies have offices in St. Moritz.

These situations constantly are in flux so when you are planning this itinerary just be aware to check which car rental companies have a rental station at the appropriate towns, unlimited mileage policies, hours that the rental office is open, etc.

Once you have dropped off your rental car return to the train station in Brig to board the Glacier Express.

HOTEL MARGNA

Seats cannot be reserved for the train itself, but the dining reservations are made in advance and unless you have done so you might not be able to enjoy the fun of having lunch in the wooden paneled, Victorian decor, dining room. Therefore call the Glacier Express as soon as you arrive in Switzerland to confirm a table. If you have not made advance luncheon reservations then as soon as you board the train, go directly to the dining car or ask the conductor if there are still tables available. You are certain to enjoy the ride on the Glacier Express. It is expensive but it is such a unique experience that it is worth the charge. The Glacier Express wanders over a gorgeous mountain route and the scenery can be enjoyed by all since no one will have to concentrate on the drive and negotiate three high mountain passes.

It will be early evening when you arrive in St Moritz. Pick up your rental car for the approximate twenty minute drive south to Sils-Baselgia. This stopover was chosen instead of St. Moritz because the town, in my estimation, has so much more charm. St. Moritz is very famous and beautifully situated, but there is so much new and modern construction that the cozy, small Swiss town ambiance is gone. Instead drive the short distance to Sils and stay at the sophisticated but charming *MARGNA HOTEL*. The hotel is near the very quaint little towns of Sils-Maria and Sils-Baselgia (you can walk to both from the hotel.) The hotel is built on a narrow and densely wooded thread of land running between Silser-See and Silverplaner-See. Both of these small picturesque lakes are beautiful and add a gorgeous foreground to the overshadowing, magnificent mountains which surround the entire valley. Once a patrician home of a "homesick" Engadineer, Johann Josty, the beautiful Margna Hotel is not a simple rustic inn, but rather benefits from the amenities that a large, deluxe hotel can offer without losing the feeling of intimacy. Antiques are everywhere plus colorful bouquets of flowers. As in each of the mountain retreats in this itinerary the Sils area is a perfect headquarters for hiking in summer and skiing in winter. Because the two lakes are so close to the hotel, the summer also offers boat rides on the lake, wind surfing and fishing, etc. All in all a delightful stopover.

Only about an hour and a half from Sils is Klosters after a very scenic drive
following the Inn River Valley north through St. Moritz, Samedan and Zuoz.
Zuoz has a colorful main square with a fountain in the middle and is a nice place
to break your journey. The fountain is a bear standing on its hind legs and was
the emblem of the Plantas family, prominent in the history of this region. Also in
the town are many beautifully preserved Engadine style buildings of heavily
plastered walls painted in various colors decorated with flowers, shields or
geometric designs.

CHESA GRISHUNA

After Zuoz, just before Susch, turn left and go over the Fluelapass. As you drop down to the next valley in the distance is the city of Davos. A famous ski resort, Davos originally developed as a health spa and is now a maze of high rise buildings to accommodate the winter crowds. On its outskirts is a lovely lake - The Davoser See. In summer the promenade around the lake is obviously a favorite of many strollers.

Just beyond Davos the road drops down into the Lanquart Valley. The village of Klosters is encompassed by the rugged Silvretta Mountain peaks. They are magnificent in their splendor, contrasting dramatically with the valley which is soft and gentle. In the fall new-mown meadows, velvet green in color, await the return of cattle from their alpine pastures. The setting is very peaceful and extremely scenic.

The town of Klosters backs up to the same mountains as Davos and actually the two ski areas interconnect like a giant spider web. Although Klosters is also a new town in the sense that most of the construction has been completed in recent years the town has grown with a gracious style encompassing the Swiss chalet motif into its many lovely shops and restaurants. The town is very well situated for hiking in the summer or skiing in the winter. The train station is also the terminus for a cableway up the mountain. Klosters is also famous as a center for ice skating and tobogganing. However it is in summer that Klosters is most regal in her beauty. There are many hotels in Klosters but my favorite is the *CHESA GRISHUNA*, a small chalet style hotel only about a block from the railroad station. The hotel is a family operation, attentively and lovingly owned and managed by the Guler Family. The Chesa Grishuna oozes with old world charm combining antiques, old beams, copper and flowers with great taste. The dining room is superb and the food, graciously and professionally served, is excellent.

From Klosters it is only about a half an hours drive until you meet the freeway to continue on to Zurich or Lucerne.

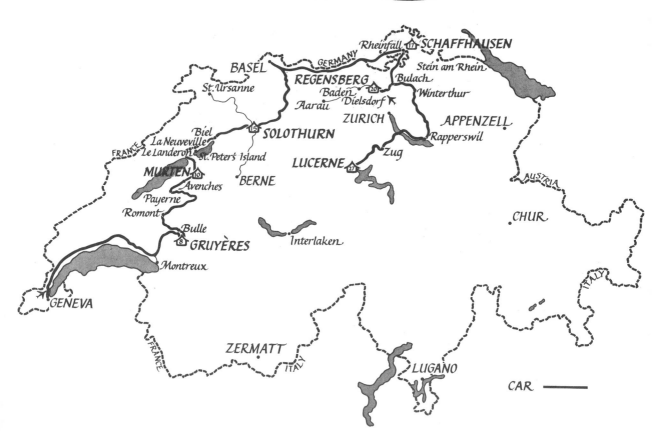

Medieval Villages

Rheinfall SCHAFFHAUSEN

BASEL GERMANY

Stein am Rhein

St. Ursanne REGENSBERG Bülach

Baden Winterthur

Aarau Dielsdorf

ZURICH APPENZELL

Biel SOLOTHURN Rapperswil

La Neuveville FRANCE

Le Landeron St. Peter's Island Zug

MURTEN LUCERNE

Avenches BERNE

Payerne CHUR

Romont

Bulle Interlaken

GRUYÈRES

Montreux

GENEVA

ZERMATT FRANCE

ITALY LUGANO

AUSTRIA

ITALY

CAR ———

SWITZERLAND HAS SOME OF the most enchanting and remarkably well preserved medieval villages in Europe. Scattered across her countryside are towns whose character and atmosphere allude to a style of life that slipped by many centuries ago. Walled ramparts often enclose a maze of twisting, narrow streets, stone buildings, painted fountains, intricate clock towers, turrets and a wealth of history. Sometimes capping the crest of a hill or perched precariously on a valley's ledge, these villages captivate the imagination and are fascinating to explore.

This itinerary wanders from Lucerne to Geneva through gorgeous countryside and intriguing medieval towns. It would be excellent for the "second time around" traveler who has already followed the standard tourist trail between Zurich and Geneva via Lucerne and Interlaken and who would like to discover Switzerland with a different approach and emphasis. This itinerary would also dovetail quite well and complete a "circle trip" by hinging on to the "Swiss highlights" itinerary that begins in Zurich and ends Geneva.

The true "medieval village Connoisseur" among you will say that many of the walled villages have been left out. This is true. There are many others scattered throughout Switzerland, but these are some of my favorites and are spaced in such a way as to map a delightful journey.

DESTINATION I : LUCERNE *WILDEN MANN HOTEL*

With an enchanting setting, Lucerne is a delightful starting point for this itinerary since it serves as a wonderful introduction to Switzerland and offers a tempting sampling of what is to come - lakes, mountains, a twisting river, wonderful bridges, colorful flowers, fountains, boats, decorative buildings, and beautifully preserved old towns.

Remnants of stone walls serve to trace an outline around the old town of Lucerne. Although the ramparts which once encircled the city have deteriorated with time, the old section remains a marvelously preserved example of a medieval city, an exceptionally attractive one. A river winds through the town as it meanders down to the lake. The river banks are lined with stately old buildings and are frequently connected by architecturally lovely old bridges. Built in the fourteenth century, the Kapellbrucke is a covered wooden bridge, painted in murals, with even a little chapel at its midway point, and has almost become a trademark of Lucerne.

To compliment the theme of this itinerary the *WILDEN MANN* is both a logical and delightful choice for a hotel. It is located right in the center of the old town and dates back to the beginning of the sixteenth century.

Fascinating are the series of scenes in the dining room of the Wilden Mann. Encased in a frame of glass, these are a series of miniature scenes depicting the Wilden Mann from its early days until now. Look carefully and you will see in the first scene an actual drawbridge in front of the hotel. As the centuries progressed the moat was covered over and and replaced by a street.

WILDEN MANN HOTEL

DESTINATION   II :   REGENSBERG   *ROTE ROSE*

From Lucerne head north towards Zurich. You might want to deviate from the highway about twenty minutes after leaving Lucerne to stop at the town of Zug located at the north end of the Zuger-See (Lake Zug). Zug is a very old city with many buildings dating back to the fifteenth century. There is a small core within the old city which is still a perfectly walled enclave. It is entered through a gateway under the clock tower. Soon after leaving Zug change directions and follow a road heading south along the Zurich See and watch for signs to Rapperswil. Located on a small peninsula that juts out into Lake Zurich, the town is definitely worth a stop. Rapperswil has a wonderful location on the banks of the lake, many colorful squares and exceptionally preserved medieval buildings. A majestic castle, on a rise in the middle of town, contains an art museum, the Polish Museum. During World War II many of the art treasures of Poland were smuggled out of the country and brought here for safe keeping. Many still remain and are on display at the museum.

From Rapperswil continue north for approximately thirty minutes to Winterthur. This is quite a large commercial city, but the central section still retains a great deal of medieval charm. The most interesting section is located near the train station. One of the main streets has been closed to all but pedestrian traffic. A variety of shops are housed in quaint medieval buildings and only a short walk further on is one of the most famous museums in Switzerland, the Galerie Oskar Reinhart. This is truly an exquisite small museum. It houses works by the famous European artists from the eighteenth to the twentieth century, with the paintings beautifully displayed in lovely natural lighting. Especially enjoyable are the paintings by Anker who captured the warmth and charm of family life in Switzerland in the same way that Carl Larsen did in Sweden. The museum is usually closed on Monday mornings and from Noon to 2 PM.

From Winterthur head west toward Bulach - about a twenty minute drive. Upon arrival in Bulach follow carefully the signs heading west towards Dielsdorf - another ten minutes beyond Bulach. The town of Regensberg is just on the western outskirts of Dielsdorf, perched on a nearby hilltop.

Regensberg is very, very special. Within only a few miles of Zurich is this perfectly preserved medieval village "icing" the knoll of a small hill. Vineyards climb up to the little town whose atmosphere takes you back five hundred years. Lodged in this romantic village is one of the most exquisite little inns in Switzerland, the *ROTE ROSE*. The Rote Rose is owned by the world famous rose artist, Lotte Gunthart, and is managed by her delightful daughter, Christa Schafer.

ROTE ROSE

As the Rote Rose has only two one-bedroom suites, reservations are strongly recommended. A couple of days could easily be devoted to this area. A day would be well spent exploring the tiny town of Regensberg itself, enjoying the comfort of the Rote Rose and sampling the menu of the Gunthart's gourmet Krone Restaurant. Lotte Gunthart's art gallery is in the Rote Rose and open in the afternoons from 2PM to 6PM except Sundays and holidays. It is possible to spend several hours here if you are want to purchase some rose prints as the selection is quite large. Also available at the shop are many books on roses, lovely note paper and rose motif gift items.

An excursion to circle some of the walled villages in the Regensberg area might also prove of interest. It is only about a twenty minute drive to the ancient spa town of Baden. As you approach Baden it looks like a rather industrial town, but be patient and head for the core of the old village. On the banks of the Limmat River, Baden has many wonderful old gaily painted houses with steep roofs and dormer windows. The houses step down the hillside in columns until the last row becomes the river bank itself. A covered wooden bridge sets a picturesque scene at the middle of the old section of town and a church with a high steeple sets the backdrop to the picture. This spa town of Baden has been famous since Roman times and its water especially popular for the treatment of arthritis.

From Baden drive on to Aarau, another beautifully preserved medieval town. Like Baden, as you approach the town it looks like an industrial city, as indeed it is - being famous for textiles. However, the center of the old town is delightful with narrow twisting streets, colorful houses with steep brown roofs, frequently with fresco decorations under the eaves, and carved little bay windows jutting out over the tiny streets. Aarau is a perfect town for strolling.

I am sure Christa Schafer, the hostess at the Rote Rose, can add her favorites of other excursions to take from Regensberg if you can tear yourself away from your own snug little apartment - your own little castle on a hill!

As the drive is very short make a leisurely departure from Regensberg and still arrive in time for lunch at your hotel in Schaffhausen. *RHEINHOTEL FISCHERZUNFT* is aptly named because it has a superb location right on the pedestrian promenade running along the Rhine. There is interesting sightseeing in the Schaffhausen area and the Rheinhotel, managed by the owners Andre and Doreen Jaeger-Soong, is a delightful place to stay.

The town of Schaffhausen is a well preserved, walled, medieval city. It developed as a result of the Rhine River traffic and resultant commerce. To the west of town is the Rheinfall, (water fall) . It halted the flow of river traffic and arrangements had to be made to circumvent the falls and transport the cargo by land. Schaffhausen grew to accommodate the delays and trade. In town are a number of painted houses with quaint projecting windows called "oriel" windows. There are also several delightful fountains, old towers, and of course, a castle on a knoll above the city.

While in Schaffhausen you will certainly want to make the very short excursion to see the Rheinfall. Where the falls come cascading down there is a park and a concession where you can take a boat right out to the bottom of the falls.

Another excursion from Schaffhausen would be to visit the walled town of Stein am Rhein. It is packed with tourists during the summer season, but it looks like a fairy tale village with each building almost completely covered in colorful paintings and designs. An option would be to take the ferry from Schaffhausen to Stein am Rhein for lunch and make it a day's outing. Ferry schedules are available at the Rheinhotel Fischerzunft.

RHEINHOTEL FISCHERZUNFT

DESTINATION   IV :   SOLOTHURN   *HOTEL KRONE*

The medieval city of Basel is a convenient stop on the way to Solothurn. Basel, in spite of its size, still retains a wonderful ambiance of old world charm. The old section of town is easily seen as you drive into town and identified by the two towering spires of the cathedral. From the Munster Platz you can explore most of the old section on foot.

From Basel it is a short and easy drive to Solothurn. Solothurn might appear unattractive on the outskirts, however, once you pass through the medieval wall the modern world is left behind and you enter a sector of the town that transports you back through the centuries. You should not have a problem finding the *KRONE HOTEL*. It is on one of the main streets and faces the plaza in front of the large cathedral of St. Ursen. The bedrooms in the main building are large and airy, while the rooms in the newer section are very small. Splurge and ask for one of the more spacious rooms - the difference is worth it. The main dining room at the Krone is charming and always busy with not only tourists but with the local citizens. The Krone seems to be the center for much of the social life in town with wedding receptions, business meetings, and parties.

The town of Solothurn is one of the oldest Roman settlements in the Alps. With many squares, fountains, and colorful buildings it is a fun town for meandering. It will not take you long to really see the whole city so I would suggest some other sightseeing excursions from Solothurn. One day drive up into the Jura mountains to visit the little walled town of St-Ursanne. You enter the completely walled town by crossing the river and passing through the quaint gates. St-Ursanne is located in a beautiful section of Switzerland famous for the breeding of colts. In the summer there are rolling green meadows with splendid looking horses grazing.

Another excursion from Solothurn would be to travel to the town of Berne. The old section of the city is magnificent with whimsical fountains, colorful squares, arcaded shops, and perfectly preserved medieval buildings. Another side trip is the thirty five minute ferry ride to the stork colony of Altreu.

HOTEL KRONE

DESTINATION   V :   MURTEN   *VIEUX MANOIR AU LAC*

Although, only a very short drive from Solothurn to Murten, there are a couple of walled villages along the way. From Solothurn take the highway west toward Biel. Biel is another picturesque medieval town, however if time is short it might be best to bypass Biel and continue directly on to the tiny town of La Neuveville, a perfectly preserved, walled village on the banks of Biel Lake. Near La Neuveville is St. Peter's Island, where Jean-Jacques Rousseau stayed in 1765. It is possible to visit the island and see the house where he lived by taking a boat from La Neuveville. Further along the shore from Neuveville is another marvelous, miniature walled village, Le Landeron. In summer both Le Landeron and La Neuveville are delightful with masses of flowers, picturesque buildings, brightly painted fountains, clock towers, little shops, and outside cafes. Do not linger too long because your next and final destination is another and even more striking walled town, Murten.

Murten, snuggled along the banks of Lake Murten, is a fairytale village. The best vantage point for viewing the town is from the top of the ramparts that surround it. The town deserves to be lazily wandered to fully enjoy the twisting little streets, fountains, old buildings, and little squares.

Settle tonight at *LE VIEUX MANOIR AU LAC*, located on the lake shore only about a half mile to the south of Murten. An old manor house set in its own beautiful gardens, the hotel is a relaxing spot to stay, perhaps to take some countryside walks. The food is absolutely delicious and impeccably served. The bedrooms vary in size and decor but they are all nice. Try for a room overlooking the lake.

VIEUX MANOIR AU LAC

DESTINATION   VI: GRUYERES *HOSTELLERIE DES CHEVALIERS*

The picturesque town of Gruyeres is just a short drive along the main highway from Murten. To extend your journey and include some sightseeing into your day, I would suggest the following deviations. First, instead of returning to the main highway, drive south along Lake Murten. Soon after you pass the south end of the lake you come to the town of Avenches. It is hard to believe as you look at this sleepy little hamlet of about 2,000 inhabitants that it was once a powerful Roman city boasting a population over 20,000 in the first and second centuries. You can grasp the mood of this "lost city" of the Romans when you visit the ampitheatre built to seat 10,000. In a tower over the ampitheater's entrance is a museum displaying some of the artifacts found in the excavations plus an interesting pottery collection.

Another excursion enroute to Gruyeres would be to travel just south of Avenches to the town of Payerne and visit its famous eleventh century Abbey. This Benedictine Abbey is supposed to have been founded by the Empress Adelheid, wife of the Emperor Otto I. The church is one of the finest examples of Romanesque architecture in Switzerland with simple lines, but marvelous proportions and use of golden limestone and grey sandstone.

Romont, a small walled, medieval town, is also on the way to Gruyeres. To reach Romont it is necessary to travel the small country roads leading south east from Payerne. It is only about a half an hour beyond Payerne. The town was built by Peter II of Savoy in the thirteenth century and has a very picturesque site on the knoll of a hill overlooking the Glane Valley. From Romont continue southeast on the small road toward Bulle. Just beyond Bulle the small town of Gruyeres will appear just ahead of you crowning the top of a miniature mountain.

To reach Gruyeres you wind up the little road toward the village, but you cannot take your car into the town itself as it is closed to traffic. However there are several car parks located as you near the town. The *HOSTELLERIE DES CHEVALIERS* is located just above the car park at the entrance to the town. As you look at the hotel from the parking area the hotel appears pleasant but nothing special. However, looks are deceiving because although the entrance to the hotel is simple, the rooms in the rear of the hotel open out to a lovely mountain vista. The dining rooms of the hotel are in an entirely separate building situated to the right of the hotel section. Although the bedrooms are simple, the dining areas are really spectacular. There are several dining rooms, each done in a different color scheme and decor, and each beautiful. Many antiques are used, plus of course, the ever present tradition of fresh flowers everywhere. The chef is famous for his culinary art and guests come from far and near.

HOSTELLERIE DES CHEVALIERS

Gruyeres is such a beautiful little town that is attracts bus loads of visitors who crowd the small main street during the day. However, most of the tourists leave at night and the town returns to its fairytale quality. Return in the evening to the idyllic Swiss village and the town is "yours" to enjoy. Plan excursions during the day to avoid the bustle of the midday tourist rush. One possible outing would be to go to the small museum-factory just at the bottom of the hill from Gruyeres. Housed in a modern building the exterior is painted with a pastural scene, and is difficult to miss. In the factory demonstrations are given as to how cheeses are made in the various Swiss cantons. There is also a movie, given in an English version, with an explanation of the process. Cheese enthusiasts might want to linger in this area and take other short excursions to visit other little villages and sample their dairy products...You might come home a little plumper, but a connoisseur of the marvelous varieties of the delicious Swiss cheeses.

Other sidetrips that might be appealing would be to travel the distance to Lake Geneva and explore the many quaint little towns along the lake. Plus, of course the ever pleasurable rides on the lake can be picked up from most of the lakeside towns. Also, from Gruyeres you can easily visit the famous Chillon Castle which is located on a tiny peninsula near Montreux. This castle originally belonged to the Counts of Savoy but its great fame came from Lord Byron's famous poem "The Prisoner of Chillon."

When it is time to leave Gruyeres there are several options. It is just a short drive around Lake Geneva to Geneva where there are train connections all over Europe plus international flights if you must return home. Or it is also a very easy trip to complete your "Medieval" circle and return to Lucerne via the beautiful Simmental Valley, stopping along the way to visit the walled town of Thun.

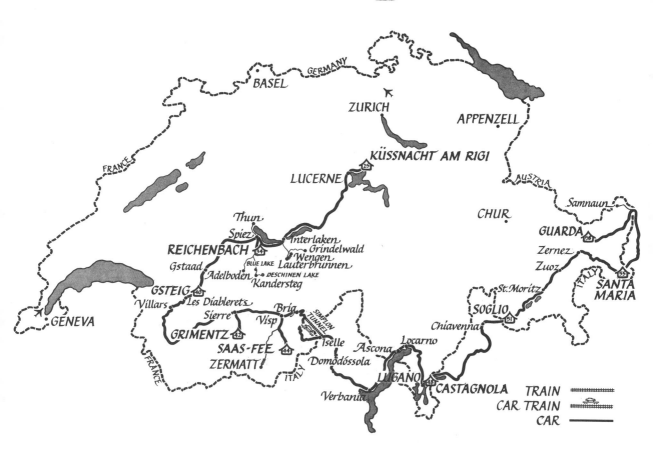

THIS ITINERARY WAS ALMOST never written. It was long after the outline for the book had been finalized that the decision was made to include it. As the itinerary's route and theme developed it seemed a natural!

Barbara, our illustrator, was studying brochures to assist her with the hotel sketches. She inquired as to the reason for not including the Fischer's Seehotel in Castagnola. After explaining that it was not quite the "calibre" of the other hotels in the book, that the brochure was for reference purposes only, the hotel was simple and not an architectural masterpiece or reeking with "country charm", she asked me the price. It was incredibly low. "Oh you must include it", she said. "This is just the type of hotel my husband Richard and I would adore. Our budget would stretch so much further. We could stay a week with meals for what a few days would cost in some of the other inns for room only." Barbara asked if I had others in the inexpensive category that were not going to be included. Actually I had been intrigued by several small inns found off the beaten path, such as the Hotel Palazzo Salis in Soglio, the Hotel Baren in Gsteig, the Hotel du Moiry in the medieval village of Grimentz. Barbara's enthusiasm for the qualities of these "little gems" was contagious. So this itinerary is for my friend Barbara and for others, young at heart, adventurous in spirit and traveling on a budget. Have Fun!

This itinerary begins at Kussnacht am Rigi, a small village located on the northern tip of Lake Lucerne. A convenient spot to begin your journey as Lucerne is just a short drive away. For a change of pace and an alternative to driving you might decide to take advantage of a ferry service between the two towns. The *HOTEL DU LAC SEEHOF* is situated right by the ferry landing and is managed by the fifth generation of the Trutmann Family. The bedrooms are all without private bath, very simple in decor, but pleasingly spacious. Located on the water's edge the views from the terrace create a delightful atmosphere. This is a perfect example of a pleasing compromise. Linger over a romantic dinner and know that the setting more than makes up for the fact that the bathroom is located "down the hall"!

HOTEL DU LAC SEEHOF

The drive from Kussnacht am Rigi to Reichenbach is beautiful passing by Lake Brienz and Lake Thun, two lakes connected by a bridge of land on which sits the town of Interlaken. This area provides a wealth of lovely mountain vistas all the way to Reichenbach. Stop along the way for lunch on the lakeside to enjoy the view.

GASTHOF BAREN

Reichenbach is a small town in the Kandertal Valley, only about fifteen minutes drive after the turnoff from the south side of the Thuner See near the town of Spiez. You will have no problem finding the *GASTHOF BAREN*. The town is small and it should be easy to spot this especially attractive wooden chalet type building with a sign showing the figure of a bear (Baren means "bear"). This inn is actually more famous as a restaurant than as a hotel, and justifiably so. The food is excellent. The owner, Mr Murner, is also the chef and a delightful host. The Murner Family is very involved in the management of the Gasthof Baren and their presence makes this stopover rise from a nice interlude to a very special experience. The price of the simple bedrooms, all without baths, is very reasonable. Mr Murner speaks perfect English and he will be happy to assist you with ideas for hiking or sightseeing while you are at the Hotel Baren.

With Reichenbach as your base it is an easy journey to Interlaken. For a day's excursion combine a trip to Interlaken with the Jungfrau circuit or perhaps with a trip to the medieval town of Thun. A lake excursion from either Interlaken or Thun is always enjoyable. At Thun a very dramatic castle perched on the hill overlooks the town. A covered wooden staircase leading up to the castle makes it not only fun but an adventure to visit. If it is time to consider gifts Thun has an interesting shopping street with a mall of shops on an upper level and an elevated sidewalk.

After visiting Thun or a lake excursion on either Lake Thun or Lake Brienz, consider exploring the road that leads to the end of the Kandertal Valley. For this trip travel beyond Reichenbach to the south. Along the way are signs for the Blausee or Blue Lake which is a gorgeous little lake. Follow the wooded, scenic pathway to the exotic blue lake, surrounded by mass of rocks plus in the distance the scenic mountain backdrop. One wonders how nature can compose such magic. On the side of the lake is a perfect chalet restaurant. The Blausee is very popular and will be crowded if the day is nice - especially with families since this little lake especially appeals to the little ones. Continuing beyond the Blausee you come to the town of Kandersteg. The road actually ends in this typical Swiss Village with a splendid setting of meadows and towering mountains. From here a mountain rail pass is the only access over to the Rhone Valley. However, there is access by a chairlift, found across the bridge, rising up to Lake Oeschinen, a beautiful high mountain lake surrounded by cliffs and again with a spectacular mountain backdrop.

DESTINATION   III :   GSTEIG   *HOTEL BAREN*

Gsteig is only a few miles south of the "jet set" town of Gstaad. The advantage of Gsteig is that price does not govern the setting and it shares the same beautiful mountain valley as Gstaad. Actually the small town of Gsteig is quainter and more scenic than Gstaad. It does not have the many shops and restaurants associated with its fancy neighbor. To reach Gsteig return to the main highway from the Kandersteg Valley and then almost immediately turn off to follow the Simmental Valley west toward Gstaad. At Saanen take the road toward Gstaad. Gsteig is just about ten minutes from Gstaad.

When you reach Gsteig you cannot miss the *HOTEL BAREN* on the main street near the small church. The building facade is such a marvelous example of the intricate carvings characteristic of the Oberland region that the hotel is protected by the government as a "national treasure". The town of Gsteig is custodian of the hotel and selects the management. The dark wooden gables of the Gasthof Baren are covered in detailed designs and in summer the window boxes are filled with flowers and are a mass of color. The bedrooms are extremely simple and without private bathrooms. However, the dining room is not only especially cozy and attractive, but also is well known for its food.

You will love a few days exploring this tiny valley of such great beauty. There are many wonderful trails for hiking in the summer plus in winter there is the world famous skiing at nearby Gstaad. It is also only a short trip over to the town of Gruyeres. This charming little "picture book" medieval village hugs a small hilltop. The town is really only one main street full of picturesque buildings plus a magnificent setting. In summer the meadows are incredibly green and seem to flow up to the mountains - it is a scene for Heidi! The town is famous for its excellent cheeses and creams as Gruyeres is in one of the excellent dairy sections of Switzerland. If you go to Gruyeres be sure to stop at the Hostellerie St. Georges or one of the other restaurants for some quiche and, when in season, some berries with the unbelievably thick cream.

HOTEL BAREN

Your next stop is the tiny town of Grimentz. The drive from Gsteig to Grimentz is beautiful but involves mountainous driving and the route is only recommended after the snows are off the passes. Until winter has subsided bypass Grimentz and go directly on to the next destination in the itinerary, Saas-Fee. When clear follow the road which climbs steadily from the valley after you leave Gsteig. It twists over the mountains, passes through the town of Les Diablerets, the ski resort of Villars and then winds down into the Rhone Valley. Upon reaching the main highway turn east. At Sierre follow the signs to Grimentz.

HOTEL DU MOIRY

The town of Grimentz nestles on a side of the mountain overlooking the valley and beyond to the high mountain peaks. The village is a masterpiece of perfection with almost all of the buildings constructed in the traditional Valais style with dark weathered wood, slate roofs and balconies. All this is set off in summer by masses of brilliant red geraniums. The *HOTEL DU MOIRY*, found on the edge of town, is quite simple, but for the location, an excellent value.

The Grimentz area is wonderful for high mountain walking. It is possible to hike to neighboring villages. If you become tired, or if the wine with lunch along the way makes you lazy, you can always take the postal bus back to Grimentz!

DESTINATION V: SAAS-FEE *WALDHOTEL FLETSCHHORN*

Take time for a morning stroll or a leisurely breakfast as the drive from Grimentz to Saas-Fee is very short. Return to the highway that traverses the Rhone Valley and head east. At Brig turn south towards Zermatt and Saas-Fee. Toward the end of the valley follow the signs for Saas-Fee. Here the road climbs up the mountain and ends up at a parking lot for Saas-Fee where you must park as cars are not allowed in town. Use a telephone at the Tourist Office to call directly to *WALDHOTEL FLETSCHHORN* and advise them of your arrival. Either Mr. Dutsch, the owner, or one of the porters will come to meet you and whisk you off in their electric cart through the town, over the open meadow, then through a thick forest path to the Waldhotel Fletschhorn. The first glimpse of the Waldhotel Fletschhorn will undoubtedly win your heart. What a sensational location! The hotel itself is not the epitome of a small Swiss chalet - rather it is simply an attractive hotel, but the setting is incredible. The hotel is located in a clearing of the forest in its own little world overlooking the Saas Valley and the majestic towering peaks of the Mischabel Mountain group.

The Waldhotel Fletschhorn is not a bargain hotel in the normal sense. However, it is included because it really is a bargain when you consider the value received. First of all, is the gorgeous location. Second, the hotel has rates which include meals and so for the price of a hotel room alone in many of the fancy resorts such as Zermatt, at the Waldhotel Fletschhorn you have "room and board" and the food is some of the best in Switzerland. Irma Dutsch has the reputation of being the finest woman chef in Switzerland. She not only oversees the preparation but actually is in the kitchen cooking each delicious meal. So when you make a reservation by all means sign up for demi-pension (breakfast and dinner) or better yet for full pension (three meals a day).

WALDHOTEL FLETSCHHORN

The third reason the hotel is such a great value is that your stay is also a social event. The hotel is almost like a house party where at the end of the day everyone sits around and compares their day's mountain adventures. In summer the conversations will share "favorite" hiking paths. In winter the talk will revolve around snow conditions and gorgeous views encountered on cross country ski trails. Your companions are likely to be guests very familiar with the area as the Dutsch Family has, through their special gift of hospitality, built up friends around the world who come every year. Large corporation presidents, lawyers, writers, Hollywood producers, etc. find their way to this simple but unique Shangri La.

DESTINATION VI: CASTAGNOLA *FISCHER'S SEEHOTEL*

If time permits linger in the mountains at Saas-Fee. Your next destination is also delightful but completely different overlooking a beautiful lake instead of the mountain valley.

Today's journey demands an early departure, the destination being the hotel that inspired the theme of this itinerary. The first leg of the trip is an hour drive to Brig and from there you have a choice of either driving over the Simplonpass or taking a train through the Simplon Tunnel. Unless your budget is really slim, the train is by far the easiest way to cross the mountains and a fun adventure in its own right. If you decide on the train remember to allow enough time to purchase tickets and get your car to the designated boarding point. Directional signs are very explicit. They show a car on top of a train. The trains leave on the hour to travel through the longest train tunnel in Europe. You stay in your car during the trip and jostle in total darkness until you emerge approximately twenty minutes later at the town of Iselle in Italy. Although, there is a "short cut" to the Swiss-Italian Lakes by following the turn off near Domodossola through the Vigezzo Valley, I would suggest you stay on the main highway since the road is much better. Continue on toward Verbania and then follow the shoreline of Lake

Maggiore toward Locarno and then on to Lugano. At Lugano follow the signs to the small suburb of Castagnola.

Getting to the *FISCHER'S SEEHOTEL* is not easy and yet it is the isolated setting that is responsible in part for the charm and adventure of staying here. Located on a walking path between the town of Castagnola and the town of Gandria, the hotel is not accessible by car. It requires either a ten minute walk from Castagnola or a ferry ride from Lugano. The Fischer's Seehotel is perched on the water's edge and the ferry stops only minutes away. With a little luck you can have a room overlooking the lake and awaken each morning and soak in the gorgeous view or go to bed each night and watch the lights twinkling across the lake. This is a simple hotel, nothing dramatic in its looks, but what a location, and so very reasonably priced. A week's stay here, including meals is comparable in price to a couple of nights at some of the deluxe hotels along the lake....and not one of them could offer a more spectacular setting!

Linger in the Lake District for as long as time permits for there is truly so much to see and do. Take the boat into Lugano which still maintains in its central core a charming medieval village with excellent shops and restaurants. Or drive over to Ascona, where behind the main street are twisting little streets with more shops and restaurants. From Castagnola take the ferry to the little town of Morcote and have lunch at the restaurant of the Carina Hotel perched over the water. For another outing would be to visit the Villa Favorita just a short stroll from your hotel in Castagnola. This is one of the finest museums in Switzerland with European masterpieces. It is a private museum and the hours are flexible.

FISCHER'S SEEHOTEL

DESTINATION   VII :   SOGLIO   *PALAZZO SALIS*

If your holiday time has run out then you could conveniently end your vacation in Castagnola. You are just a short drive to the international airport at Milan or a pleasant train ride back to Zurich. However, if you can squeeze in a few more days there is high adventure ahead. In fact, the south-eastern region of Switzerland (the Grisons) offers some of the most spectacular scenery in the world.

Leave Lugano driving east into Italy. At the town of Menaggio turn north and drive along Lake Como. At the north end of the lake take the highway north toward the town of Chiavenna. The Swiss border appears just a few miles past Chiavenna and Soglio appears high above you. This little town is one of the most dramatically beautiful in all of Switzerland, picture perfect - typifying the classic image of a Swiss alpine setting. A tiny village of just a few streets, the skyline dominated by a church spire, Soglio clings to a ledge high above the Bondasca Valley and looks across to jagged peaks, whose moods are affected dramatically by the day and weather. Early morning light leaves a sliver of gold on the snowy escarpment, and shifting clouds and the darkness of a mid-summer storm leaves the rugged horizon fierce and threatening.

HOTEL PALAZZO SALIS

The *PALAZZO SALIS*, a former mansion of the Salis Family, a prominent family for centuries in the Grisons, is now a hotel and marvelous value. Although the accommodations are extremely simple in their decor and without private baths, the impression of an affluent era gone by survives with antiques in the public rooms. In the upper hall there are various shields, swords and portraits on display. The dining room is very attractive with mountain water colors on the walls...plus excellent food on the table! No one seemed to speak any English when I was at the hotel, however, the graciousness of the owner, Mrs Cadisch, crossed the language barrier. With some sign language and a smile, communicating should not prove a problem.

Soglio is so spectacular that it deserves several days. There is not much to do in the village itself, but if time affords, linger here, relax, venture on a hike or two and soak in the splendors and beauty of the setting.

DESTINATION   VIII :   SANTA MARIA   *CHASA CAPOL*

To leave Soglio twist back down the narrow road leading to the valley below and turn onto the highway in the direction of St Moritz. Famous first as a health spa it is now considered the playground resort of the wealthy. From St Moritz continue north with the Engadine Valley as a guide. Zuoz is a small medieval village along the way. As you head east from Zernez the road travels through the heavily forested Swiss National Park, over the Ofenpass and then down into the unspoilt rural beauty of the Mustair Valley. Stretched along the sweep of the valley are a number of dear hamlets. Santa Maria appears at the bottom of the Ofenpass and the *CHASA CAPOL HOTEL* is located almost at the eastern end of the town. Dating back to the eighth century, this little inn is truly unique. In addition to a hotel it houses a theater, chapel and a remarkable wine cellar. The hotel is owned by the Schweizer family who are involved in the management and supervision of the restaurant. The dining and service are special. The bedrooms are simple in their decor and although rates are not as low as other hotels on this "budget" itinerary, they are an excellent value. The Chasa Capol is a delightful site for exploring the Mustair Valley and for taking advantage of the many miles of unspoilt trails in the nearby Swiss National Park.

HOTEL CHASA CAPOL

DESTINATION   IX :   GUARDA   *HOTEL MEISSER*

A few miles beyond Santa Maria the Mustair Valley flows into Italy and then loops back across the Swiss border. Following this suggested route saves backtracking along the same road. After crossing the border the route heads north just a few miles beyond customs and again across another border into Austria. Shortly after it travels back into the Engadine Valley. This might sound confusing, but as you can see by the itinerary map very few miles are actually involved and it is an easy trip. The other advantage to this route is that it travels near Samnaun, a town located near the Austrian border soon after reentering Switzerland. Samnaun's biggest attraction is completely tax free shopping. "Zoll Frei", the prices are incredible and people come from all over to purchase Austrian and Swiss clothing, hiking equipment and ski gear.

HOTEL MEISSER

The final destination for this itinerary is in the Upper Engadine Valley. Driving the valley from the east you will pass the famous spa town of Bad Scoul and then soon after the medieval town of Guarda appears perched on a ledge above the valley, very similar to Soglio. The views are spectacular and the opportunity exists for some marvelous walks.

On its own terrace overlooking the valley and mountains is the *HOTEL MEISSER*. A simple hotel, reasonably priced, the dining room is most attractive and the panoramas exceptional.

Wishing you glorious weather while in Guarda as the main recreation is to be outdoors enjoying the spectacular vistas. There is however a little sightseeing which can also be included. Nearby is Tarasp Castle crowning a tiny mountain in the valley below Guarda. The castle is extremely picturesque and there are guided tours during the summer months. (Check at the hotel to see what times the castle is open to the public.) Bad Scuol has been famous for its spas for many years and it is still possible to enjoy the public baths. Also near Guarda, on the side of the mountain above the valley, is the tiny town of Sent famous for its many buildings decorated with intricate line drawings.

This itinerary ends at Guarda. From here it is an easy half days drive back to Zurich or Lucerne.

Switzerland: By Train, Boat & Bus

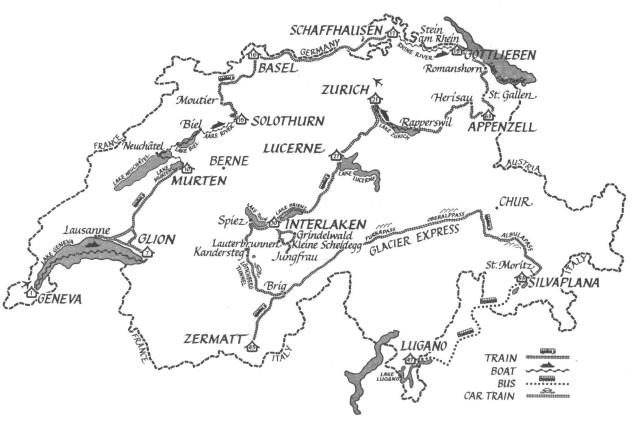

SCHAFFHAUSEN · Stein am Rhein · GOTTLIEBEN
GERMANY · RHINE RIVER · Romanshorn
BASEL
Moutier · ZURICH · Herisau · St. Gallen
Biel · SOLOTHURN · Rapperswil · APPENZELL
FRANCE · Neuchâtel · LAKE BIEL · AARE RIVER · LAKE ZURICH
LAKE NEUCHÂTEL · LAKE MURTEN · BERNE · LUCERNE · AUSTRIA
Lausanne · MURTEN · LAKE LUCERNE · CHUR
GLION · Spiez · INTERLAKEN · OBERALPPASS
LAKE GENEVA · LAKE THUN · LAKE BRIENZ · Grindelwald · FURKAPASS · GLACIER EXPRESS · ALBULAPASS
GENEVA · Lauterbrunnen · Kleine Scheidegg · St. Moritz
Kandersteg · Jungfrau · SILVAPLANA
LÖTSCHBERG TUNNEL · Brig · ITALY
FRANCE · ZERMATT · LUGANO
ITALY · LAKE LUGANO

TRAIN
BOAT
BUS
CAR TRAIN

Of all the itineraries in the guide, this is the most exciting to me. It offers unique modes to travel Switzerland from major cities to tiny hamlets via high mountain passes, lush valleys, lakes, and rivers - all without the use of a car. Part of the charm of this itinerary is that the transportation, rather than being simply a means of travel, becomes part of the sightseeing experience. This is a long itinerary, but if your holiday time is limited it would certainly be feasible to isolate the segments that most appeal to you.

The potential of this itinerary was realized when staying in Gottlieben, a town located on the Rhine River. Noticing the ferry in front of the Hotel Krone departing to Schaffhausen, I wished I could just pick up my suitcase, climb on board and get off in front of another of my favorite hotels, the Rheinhotel Fischerzunft in Schaffhausen, a few hours later. How much more enjoyable to savor the lovely Rhine, passing along the way such glorious little towns as Stein am Rhein, rather than passing large trucks on a busy highway. In Solothurn I was surprised to notice a boat connection directly to the walled town of Murten! How delightful I thought to journey through the countryside via canals and lakes instead of by car. So I returned home eager to see if the various travel segments by land and water could be coordinated. Knowing how remarkably efficient the Swiss transportation network is, I should never have doubted the reality of this itinerary. I have not had the pleasure to follow all the boat connections suggested in this itinerary, but I will ! This itinerary is planned for my benefit as well as yours.

This itinerary does have a few prerequisites. It is geared to a leisurely pace so time must not be a problem. To hurry this particular holiday would prove frustrating and spoil the very reason it is special. Also, because some of the ferries only operate in the summer, vacation dates need to be carefully planned.

Finally, it is absolutely a must that you travel very lightly. I suggest just one tiny suitcase because cumbersome bags will be an aggravation and burden when trying to make quick connections between trains or boats and certainly diminish some of the joy of travel. So pack lightly and join me in Switzerland by train, boat and bus!

IMPORTANT NOTE:
IN THIS ITINERARY I HAVE GIVEN SUGGESTED TIMES FOR THE TRAINS, BOATS, AND BUSES. THESE ARE TO BE USED AS A GUIDELINE ONLY. YOU MUST CHECK EACH OF THE SCHEDULES LOCALLY TO VERIFY TIMES OF ARRIVAL AND DEPARTURE. SOME TRAINS, BOATS AND BUSES ONLY OPERATE ON CERTAIN DAYS OF THE WEEK OR DURING CERTAIN SEASONS OF THE YEAR AND DEPARTURES CAN VARY. I DEBATED WHETHER OR NOT TO INCLUDE THE TIMES AND SCHEDULES, BUT DECIDED THAT IT WAS IMPORTANT TO PROVIDE YOU WITH AN APPROXIMATE GUIDELINE SO THAT YOU COULD BASICALLY SEE HOW THE ITINERARY WORKS AND HOW IT ACCOMMODATES YOUR OWN TRAVEL PLANS. HOWEVER, AGAIN I WANT TO STRESS THAT YOU PERSONALLY VERIFY TRANSPORTATION SCHEDULES TO AVOID DISAPPOINTMENT.

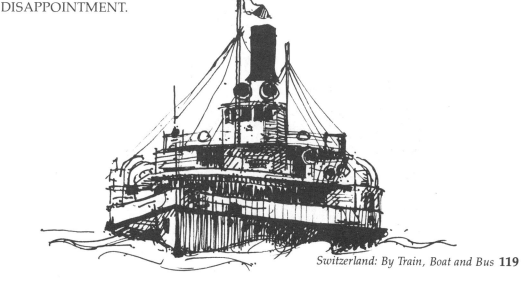

Switzerland: By Train, Boat and Bus **119**

Geneva is the first city on this itinerary. A delightful starting point for a Swiss vacation, Geneva is a lovely blend of the old and new - the medieval portion of the city rising on the hillside on the left bank of the Rhone river and the newer city stretching out with peaceful promenades on the right bank of the river. Geneva is an international city. As you stroll the lake front you hear languages from all over the world and see costumes of many nationalities. In the spring Geneva becomes a small Holland with glorious tulips blooming in every little park.

LES ARMURES

The shopping in Geneva is wonderful - antique shops tempt the purse in the old section and the most sophisticated shopper can find their haven in the beautiful shops and arcades in the newer section.

The *HOTEL LES ARMURES* is located in the old section of the city facing a small square. If you enjoy a small, quiet, well run hotel without the crush of bus loads of tour groups in the lobby, you will like Les Armures. Even though the hotel was full when I visited the lobby always seemed quiet and sedate. To the left of the lobby is a lounge with antiques and comfortable chairs. The bedrooms are small but pleasantly decorated. Request a room in the front overlooking the small park if one is available. The Hotel Les Armures is difficult to find since many of the streets in the old section of town are either closed to traffic or one way. Luckily the hotel is adjacent to St. Peter's Cathedral whose spires are an easy landmark. When you wind your way through the labyrinth to St. Peters, then you will know that you cannot be more than a block away!

DESTINATION   II :   GLION   *VICTORIA HOTEL*
_____

The journey from Geneva to the next destination, Glion, is as much a sightseeing excursion as a means of transportation. Your adventure begins at the ferry pier:

10:45AM   depart Geneva (Jardin Anglais pier) by boat
3:37PM   arrive Territet

Upon arrival in Territet there is a little tramway up to Glion which runs about every fifteen minutes.

Glion is a suburb of Montreux located high above the city. Because of the spectacular views there are many summer homes and mansions.

The *VICTORIA HOTEL* is set in its own beautiful gardens with a beautiful vista over the Lake of Geneva. Staying here you will feel like royalty. The rooms have a variety of styles. If you feel like splurging, ask for a suite redecorated in antique motif with a balcony overlooking the lake.

VICTORIA HOTEL

DESTINATION   III :   MURTEN   *LE VIEUX MANOIR AU LAC*

Although it is necessary to change trains several times between Glion and Murten, the total travel time is short and the journey beautiful.

10:43AM	depart Glion by train
10:55AM	arrive Montreux
11:06AM	depart Montreux by train
11:26AM	arrive Lausanne
12:13PM	depart Lausanne by train
1:38PM	arrive Murten

The train station is in Murten, but the *LE VIEUX MANOIR AU LAC* is located about a half a mile south on the lake at Meyriez. The Vieux Manoir Au Lac is an old manor house with a wonderful lake front location plus excellent dining.

LE VIEUX MANOIR AU LAC

Only a short walk from the inn you enter through the thick walls into Murten and are magically transported back through the years to find yourself in one of the finest little medieval villages in Switzerland. Murten is like a living museum. As you walk through the little streets there are marvelous examples of medieval buildings, clock towers, ramparts, brightly painted fountains, and quaint little squares.

DESTINATION   IV :   SOLOTHURN   *HOTEL KRONE*

Today's trip from Murten to Solothurn is like a treasure hunt as you weave your way by boat through the scenic lakes, canals, and rivers of the lovely Swiss countryside. Your adventure begins in the tiny walled village of Murten from where you take the ferry to Neuchatel then on to Biel to board the boat for the final leg of your journey on the Aare River to the dramatic walled city of Solothurn.

I stressed on the previous itineraries that time schedules MUST be carefully checked. Of all the destinations this one is the most important because the boats basically operate only in the summer and NOT ON MONDAYS. Especially unpredictable is the final leg of this adventure from Biel to Solothurn. This last small river journey usually begins operation in August. However, should your journey be earlier in the summer, you can complete this final leg by train in half an hour. Therefore, as before, use the following schedule as a reference guide only to show you approximate times and where to change boats.

| 11:15AM | depart Murten by boat |
| 12:40PM | arrive Neuchatel |

LUNCH IS SUGGESTED IN THIS PICTURESQUE MEDIEVAL TOWN

| 2:15PM | depart Neuchatel by boat |
| 4:30PM | arrive Biel |

| 5:05PM | depart Biel by boat |
| 7:20PM | arrive Solothurn |

ALTERNATE TRAIN SUGGESTION IF THE FERRY IS NOT OPERATING FROM BIEL TO SOLOTHURN

| 5:23PM | depart Biel by train |
| 5:47PM | arrive Solothurn |

How very appropriate when in the ancient town of Solothurn to stay in an old inn which perpetuates the mood of antiquity. The location of the *HOTEL KRONE* is perfect and so easy to find - facing a little square opposite the impressive St Ursus Cathedral.

Solothurn is much larger than Murten, but also a marvelously preserved, completely walled medieval city located on the Aare River. It is fascinating to walk through this ancient town so full of the colorful atmosphere of bygone years. This town is so "perfect" that it was awarded the coveted Henri Louis-Wakker Prize for excellence of renovations. From Solothurn you can also take a 35 minute boat ride along the Aare River to Altreu to visit the stork colony.

HOTEL KRONE

DESTINATION   V: BASEL   *HOTEL DREI KONIGE AM RHEIN*

Your train journey today is short.

l0:10AM   depart Solothurn by train
l0:43AM   arrive Moutier

l0:46AM   depart Moutier by train
ll:36AM   arrive Basel

There is such a famous hotel in Basel that is would be a shame to stay anywhere else. The *HOTEL DREI KONIGE* is one of the oldest inns in Switzerland, dating from 1026. This is also a very historical hotel having been the site of the famous meeting between Three Kings (Conrad II, Henry III, and Rudolf II) who drew up the treaty for the transference of territories which are now western Switzerland and southern France. This historical meeting led to the name of the hotel "Drei Konige" which means "Three Kings".

Although Basel is a large city its heart is still a medieval town filled with tiny squares, fountains, marvelously preserved old buildings, beautiful cathedrals, bridges, and many interesting museums.

HOTEL DREI KONIGE

It is a simple and quick train ride from Basel to Schaffhausen:

4:03PM	depart Basel by train
5:43PM	arrive Schaffhausen

Schaffhausen is another medieval town on the banks of the Rhine River. So often in Switzerland one finds charming towns, but not a hotel to justify a stopover. Fortunately this is not the case in Schaffhausen. The hotel here is so delightful that the hotel would almost be worthy of a visit even if the town itself were not an attraction. The *RHEINHOTEL FISCHERZUNFT* has an absolutely perfect location directly on the promenade on the banks of the Rhine River.

HOTEL FISCHERZUNFT

Just west of Schaffhausen are the famous Rhine Falls, *Rheinfall*, which made it necessary for merchants to unload their river cargo and carry it around the falls before continuing their journey up stream. Schaffhausen grew up to service this river commerce.

DESTINATION VII : GOTTLIEBEN *HOTEL KRONE*

This journey along the Rhine is wonderful! It combines a splendid boat ride through quaint river villages with the practical aspect of getting between two delightful hotels. You can take a direct ferry which takes about four hours or, you can get off the ferry in the fairy tale village of Stein am Rhein to have lunch before boarding the ferry again for the completion of your journey to Gottlieben.

9:15AM   depart Schaffhausen by boat
11:05AM   arrive Stein am Rhein

LUNCHEON STOP SUGGESTED IN THIS PICTURESQUE MEDIEVAL WALLED VILLAGE

3:40PM   depart Stein am Rhein by boat
5:26PM   arrive Gottlieben

When you arrive at Gottlieben your hotel is conveniently located just a few steps from the pier. The family Schraner-Michaeli own the Hotel Krone and are very involved with its operation. The food is excellent and beautifully served in a cozy wood paneled dining room. There is also a cafe on the banks of the river for dining outside when the days are warm. Upstairs most of the bedrooms are very simple except for a few facing the river decorated with antiques.

HOTEL KRONE

DESTINATION   VIII :   **APPENZELL**   *HOTEL SANTIS*

It is necessary to take a ferry plus several trains between Gottlieben and Appenzell. It sounds complicated, but the Swiss in their predictable fashion have tailored the connections to work like a jig saw puzzle - the connections fit together perfectly!

12:51PM	depart Gottlieben by boat
1:20PM	arrive Kreuzlingen
1:32PM	depart Kreuzlingen by train
2:30PM	arrive Romanshorn
3:02PM	depart Romanshorn by train
3:30PM	arrive St Gallen
3:56PM	depart St Gallen by train
4:43PM	arrive Appenzell

HOTEL SANTIS

In Appenzell the *HOTEL SANTIS* is located on a small square in the center of town. Typical of the style of the village of Appenzell, the Hotel Santis is gaily painted on the outside with decorative designs.

The village of Appenzell, a popular tourist destination because of its colorfully painted houses, is situated in a beautiful dairy farm area of Switzerland with soft rolling green hills dotted with enormous farm houses that are a combination of home and barn. This is the Switzerland that every little girl dreams of when she reads "Heidi".

DESTINATION IX : ZURICH *HOTEL ZUM STORCHEN*

You can take a train from Appenzell to Zurich by making connections in St Gallen and Winterthur, but it would be more fun to combine your journey into a sightseeing excursion. This trip will include the great beauty of the verdant Appenzell rolling green hills, the charm of the medieval village of Rapperswil, and the fun of arriving into the city of Zurich by steamer:

l0:00AM	depart Appenzell by train
l0:33AM	arrive Herrisau
ll:08AM	depart Herrisau by train
l2:06PM	arrive Rapperswil

You can make a direct ferry connection to Zurich, but a suggestion would be to lunch in the medieval town of Rapperswil with, if time allows, a visit of the museum in the castle which is perched on a knoll just above the center of the town. This museum contains, among other artifacts, a fascinating collection of Polish treasures brought to Switzerland for protection during World War II.

1:32PM	depart Rapperswil by boat
3:32PM	arrive Zurich

HOTEL ZUM STORCHEN

The *HOTEL ZUM STORCHEN*, over 600 years old, has an ideal site on the banks of the the Limmat river in the middle of the medieval section of Zurich. Zurich does not have the feeling of a tourist center. Instead, as you walk the streets you feel the bustle of a "real" city. Of course there are tourists, but shopping next to you in the little boutique will be the local housewife, hurrying down the promenade are businessmen on their way to work, and a couple from Zurich will probably be sitting next to you at a sidewalk cafe. Nevertheless there is a carnival atmosphere to Zurich, a gaiety to the city. From both sides of the river the old section of Zurich radiates out on little twisting streets like a cobweb. Along the lakefront are parks and gardens. From the piers there are a fascinating variety of boat excursions to little villages around the lake. Being a large city, there is an excellent selection of museums to explore.

A constant "commuter" service exists between Zurich and Lucerne taking approximately an hour. The trains leave usually a few minutes before each hour. The location of the *WILDEN MANN HOTEL* is fabulous - on Bahnhofstrasse, in the middle of the old section of Lucerne within easy walking of all points of interest. The hotel embodies all that is the best about Swiss hotels - the owner present to oversee every detail of management, excellent service from the staff, attractively decorated bedrooms, fine antiques liberally used in the public rooms, and one of the most picturesque restaurants in Lucerne serving delicious food.

WILDEN MANN HOTEL

Lucerne is a wonderful town for lingering. Just strolling the quaint streets and enjoying a snack in one of the small cafes overlooking the river can easily fill an afternoon. There are always many tourists - Lucerne's enchantment is no secret. Everyone seems happy and there is a holiday air to the city.

DESTINATION XI : INTERLAKEN *HOTEL DU LAC*

A frequent direct train service runs from Lucerne to Interlaken, usually about every two hours.

1:17PM   depart Lucerne by train
3:17PM   arrive Interlaken Ost Station

The *HOTEL DU LAC* is perfect for a train itinerary, located adjacent to the Interlaken Ost (East) station. Not only does this mean when you get off the train you are "home" but also that when you get ready to take the spectacular Jungfrau circle, the train is at your front door. When you arrive into Interlaken watch carefully for the train station. The first station you come to, the Ost station, is the one you want. Porters are right at the station to take your luggage to the hotel.

Situated on the Aare River connecting Lake Thun and Lake Brienz the Hotel du Lac is an attractive choice. The dining room windows open out onto the river where you can watch the boats and the swans drift by. The bedrooms are simple, but those that overlook the river have very nice views and some even have a small balcony. In addition to having a superb setting on a natural land bridge between Lake Brienz and Lake Thun with a backdrop of majestic mountain peaks, Interlaken is famous too as the starting point for the Jungfrau Excursion beginning at the Ost train station. On a clear day this train trip, which winds its way through the meadows and then twists its way to the top of the Jungfrau, is one of the most dramatic rides in Switzerland.

HOTEL DU LAC

The Open Air Museum of Ballenberg is an interesting sightseeing excursion from Interlaken. Ballenberg is a wonderful way to learn about the various architectural styles and the crafts of Switzerland. This development reminds me of Rockefeller's preservation of the town of Williamsburg reconstructing the crafts and style of living of the American heritage. This museum opened in 1978 and is still in the process of development. Do not wait for the completion because it will be many years before the dream of the whole project will be accomplished. Ballenberg is located in an enormous park-like setting in a meadow above Lake Brienz. Houses, grouped according to region, have been brought to the park to show the most important forms of housing and settlement.

Old ways of living and working and crafts are demonstrated. The interiors offer a glimpse into yesterday with their antique furnishings. To reach Ballenberg from Interlaken take the boat or train to Brienz. There are plans for a train from Brienz to the Park but for the moment you will need to take a bus from Brienz for the short ride.

DESTINATION XII : ZERMATT *SEILER HOTEL MONT CERVIN*

Your journey today will take you through some of the most spectacular mountain vistas in the world. How nice that you will be on the train and no one will have to miss the scenery having to concentrate on the road! This is an ideal trip by train since the section from Spiez to Brig takes the "short cut" through the Lotschberg Tunnel which is for trains only. Also, the final leg of the journey into Zermatt must be done by train since no cars are allowed into Zermatt!

10:24AM	depart Interlaken Ost by train
10:49AM	arrive Spiez
10:54AM	depart Spiez by train
12:00PM	arrive Brig
12:18PM	depart Brig by train
1:45PM	arrive Zermatt

There are no cars in Zermatt. However, in true Swiss fashion, the problem of luggage and finding your hotel is easily solved. When you arrive at the station your "coach" should be waiting. The *SEILER MONT CERVIN HOTEL*, which I suggest for your sojourn, has a stately horse drawn red carriage which will whisk you quickly through town to your hotel. In winter the carriage becomes a romantic horse drawn sleigh.

SEILER HOTEL MONT CERVIN

The Seiler Family is famous in Zermatt. They pioneered tourism in Zermatt with one of the earliest hotels, the Monte Rosa. The Seiler Family has continued in the tradition of caring for tourists and now owns several hotels in Zermatt, including the luxurious Mont Cervin located in the heart of Zermatt. From the hotel you can saunter through the main street of boutiques or walk easily to the network of trails meandering under the face of the majestic Matterhorn.

Your trip between Zermatt and St. Moritz is truly a "dream come true" for any train buff. It used to be that you had to hip hop across Switzerland changing trains at various stations to connect two of their most famous mountain areas, but a few years ago an enterprising Swiss entrepreneur connected the two towns by a private railroad. You board the little red train in the morning in Zermatt and about eight hours later you arrive in St Moritz.

LA STAILA

The train chugs over some of the highest alpine passes in Switzerland, crosses meadows, tunnels through mountains, traverses glaciers, weaves through canyons all while you relax at your picture window. There is even more if you plan ahead and make a dinner reservation. There is a dining room brimming with nostalgia - wooden paneled walls, bronze fixtures, tables set with crisp linens and fresh flowers on the tables. The train is expensive and not a part of the Swiss Rail pass, but the journey is a "train trip of a life time".

When you arrive in St. Moritz you can take a bus to Silvaplana, but since the ride is only about fifteen minutes, you might find it more convenient to just take a taxi directly from the station. Silvaplana is a small town just a few miles south of the famous jet-set resort of St. Moritz. Near the center of town is the delightful, family run, small hotel, *LA STAILA*.

DESTINATION   XIV :   LUGANO   *HOTEL TICINO*

The final leg of your journey is by bus. There is direct bus service from Silvaplana and reservations are necessary for this particular bus route. Make them in advance at any of the postal bus stations in Switzerland.

1:43PM   depart Sils-Baselgia by bus
5:45PM   arrive Lugano (Main Train station)

When you arrive into Lugano please get off at the central train station because from here you can take the little cable train right down the hill directly from the train station and almost get off in front of your hotel. If you have any questions about finding the funicular ask for directions at the tourist information center in the train station.

HOTEL TICINO

Lugano is a delightful city. Although it has grown tremendously, the core of the old town still has the atmosphere of a small medieval village. Right in the heart of the ancient section of Lugano is the marvelous little *HOTEL TICINO*, located on the tiny Piazza Cioccaro - a colorful little square closed to automobiles.

From Lugano you can either continue on into Italy for further adventures, or if you want to complete your "Swiss Circle" there is frequent direct train service to Zurich taking only about three hours.

HOTEL MAP INDEX

Hotel Descriptions, Alphabetically Listed by Town, Immediately Follow This Map

Hotel Descriptions

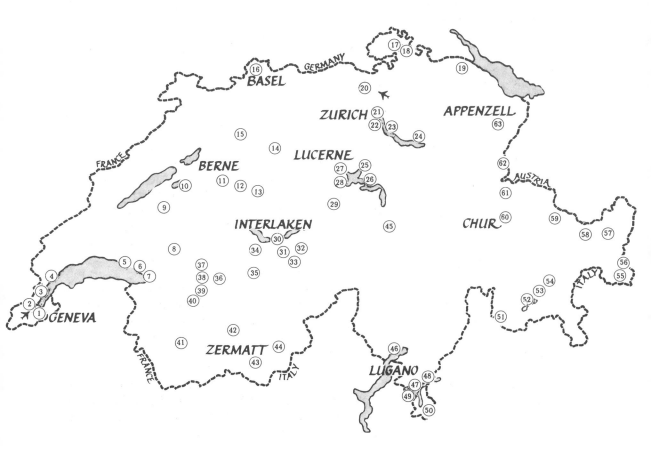

My favorable decision for this hotel was won, not by the warmth of its lobby, but rather by a smile from an absolutely enormous, curly haired St. Bernard sleeping in the middle of the floor. My gaze fell on him as I entered and I knew immediately that the Stern and Post held real possibilities! Faro is huge but gentle, affectionate, and cuddly - charming many before me. For those who lose their hearts to him, Faro plays an important role in the memory of their stay. In fact the requests for snap shots of him grew to such a proportion that finally a postcard was made of this lovable dog to send to his admirers.

Also, to welcome me was Mrs. Rosemary Tresch. She was at the front desk when I arrived. I asked her if she were the owner. She replied with a twinkle in her eye that in Switzerland the woman is not the "owner" she is always the "owner's wife"! Extremely cordial and most accommodating, Mrs. Tresch kept apologizing that she couldn't give me her undivided attention because I hadn't called for an appointment. Therefore, I was all the more appreciative that in the midst of her involvement of people checking in and the phone constantly ringing, Mrs. Tresch managed to provide many fascinating details of the Stern and Post explaining in great detail the style and decor of the rooms. Mrs. Tresch was able to show me the only unoccupied room in the hotel. Although it was charming with an antique bed and chest she advised me that only one third are done in an antique motif while the other rooms are modern, and that it is possible to specify your preference at the time you make your reservation. While the bedrooms might be sparsely decorated with antiques, they are found in abundance throughout the rest of the inn. The public rooms are inviting, very cozy and furnished with museum quality antiques.

I was impressed both with Faro, the inn and the family. Professionals in their field, the Tresch family has owned the Stern and Post for several hundred years. The current generation is involved with four other hotels in Switzerland and Mr. Tresch is personally very active in the Swiss Hotel Association.

Mrs. Tresch had many wonderful stories. I kept lingering to hear her last story of how a horse accident led to her marriage. Unfortunately, her tale was constantly being interrupted by the arrival of guests so I reluctantly departed. I will return again to the Stern and Post - I must hear the end of her story. And next time I will call ahead!

STERN and POST HOTEL
Hotelier: Family Tresch-Gwerder
Address: CH-4674 Amsteg
Phone: (044) 6 44 40   *Telex:* 866 385
Dates open: All Year, closed Wed. in winter
No. rooms: 35   *With shower/bath:* 20
Rates: Double with bath: Sfr 100-130
Credit cards: AE, VS, DC, EC
U.S.Representative: Romantik Hotels
Rep. Telephone No.: (800) 826-0015

 APPENZELL   *HOTEL SANTIS*

I highly recommend the Hotel Santis which blends beautifully into the town of Appenzell - the village of "Painted Houses". The Hotel Santis was converted into a hotel in 1853. The hotel has a varied and interesting history - it even used to house a cheese factory and a horse stable! In recent years a new wing has been added to the original building. The rooms are decorated in a variety of styles, my preference being the rooms in the original part of the hotel. They are decorated with copies of regional country style wooden furniture and quite attractive. I loved our room, number 42, which had a queen sized wooden canopy bed and a matching single bed. There was a nice desk and two chairs and, best of all, on the beds were blue and white checked comforters and plump down pillows. The public rooms seem geared to the influx of tourists who probably drop in for a mid-day meal, but the lobby offers a country welcome and the hotel has wisely insulated from the daytime activity a very peaceful and quiet lounge area.

The Santis is the epitome of what is so very special about many of the Swiss hotels - the owner is not a novice but a true professional. Joseph Heeb's pride and dedication as an owner are apparent from the friendliness of the front desk receptionist to the smile of the chambermaid, and, of course, the superb food in the dining room. The Santis has been in Mr. Heeb's family for several generations. It was owned by his grandfather and his father before him and with three sons and two daughters, the business will certainly continue to pass down within the family, hopefully for many generations to come.

HOTEL SANTIS
Hotelier: Familie J. Heeb
Address: CH-9050 Appenzell
Phone: (071) 87 26 44   *Telex:*
Dates open: February to December
No. rooms: 33   *With shower/bath:* 30
Rates: Double room: Sfr 80-130
Credit cards: AE, VS, EC
U.S.Representative: Romantik Hotels
Rep. Telephone No.: (800) 826-0015

Several years ago I discovered the Hotel Tamaro while exploring the lakeside town of Ascona. At that time I was definitely on a limited budget. I decided to return to see if the lovely little hotel of my memory was real or if I had been too influenced by the low hotel rate. Ascona remains much the same, colorful and charming. The Hotel Tamaro, ideally situated across the street from Lake Maggiore, still has cheerful little tables set out in front of the hotel attracting many who gather to enjoy a cup of coffee or an ice while leisurely watching the boats gliding in and out of the harbour. I was delighted to find the Hotel Tamaro with a fresh coat of paint and appearing even more immaculate than I remembered. It was a treat to discover several new sitting rooms; to see a cozy addition of antiques including Oriental rugs; and to view again the dining room cheerfully located in a bright sunny atrium. Awaiting me upstairs was the best surprise of all - the improvement in the decor of the bedrooms. Although neither deluxe nor oozing with antiques, they are clean, airy and pleasantly furnished. Varying in price, style and location, those at the front enjoy a lakeview and are definitely the choice rooms.

Annetta and Paolo Witzig are the owners of the Tamaro. I was sorry to miss them as I would most certainly have liked to compliment them on the beautiful job they have done in restoring and upgrading their delightful old Ticino style patrician house. The rates are still very reasonable and the Tamaro remains my favorite for Ascona.

HOTEL TAMARO
Hotelier: Annetta & Paolo Witzig
Address: CH-6612 Ascona
Phone: (093) 35 02 82   *Telex:* 846 132
Dates open: February through November
No. rooms: 56   *With shower/bath:* 45
Rates: Rooms from Sfr 55-75; with all
meals from Sfr 90-100; rates are per person
Credit cards: AE, VS, EC

 ASCONA   *CASTELLO DEL SOLE*

Like a palace situated within sprawling private grounds and beautiful scenery, the Castello del Sole has earned a five star rating and the acknowledgment of the Swiss government tourist office as among the most deluxe hotels in Switzerland. Although, smaller, cozier hotels where you soon feel like one of the family are usually my preference, this hotel will prove to be a favorite of many. Located beyond the town of Ascona in the direction of Locarno in the Lido area, the Castello del Sole (not to be confused with the Castello- Seeschloss on the main street of Ascona) is perhaps a bit difficult to find. However, if you seek luxury and a place to be properly pampered, it is well worth the effort!

The Castello del Sole is graced with elegance and a subdued formality. The atmosphere is set from the moment you enter the lobby and view the beautiful lounge areas accented with antiques and lovely paintings hung on pale colored walls. From the public rooms to the comfortable spacious bedrooms, the decorating is delightful and the professionalism and service is ever-present. The restaurant Barbarossa maintains an exceptional reputation. It specializes in using fresh products from the hotel's own farm and wines from its own vineyard!

This is a resort to tempt you for longer than an overnight stay. The Castello del Sole, although not located directly on Lake Maggiore, does have its own private beach with small boats and windsurfers. The hotel also has an indoor - outdoor swimming pool, sauna, massage facilities, five outdoor tennis courts, and two tennis courts in a magnificent tennis hall which would fulfill any tennis buff's dreams.

CASTELLO DEL SOLE
Hotelier: Mr B. Kilchenmann
Address: Via Muraccio 142
         CH-6612 Ascona
Phone: (093) 35 02 02   *Telex:* 846 138
Dates open: March through November
No. rooms: 70   *With shower/bath:* 70
Rates: Double room with bath:
     Sfr 250-320

57   **BAD SCUOL**   *HOTEL GUARDAVAL*

Although Bad Scuol is rather a hub of activity, the Hotel Guardaval is isolated from the "action". Located on a road running above the highway, it is a little world of tranquillity. Quite old, parts of the hotel date from 1691. The main building is simple in design - painted white with bright geraniums adorning the window boxes. The front reception area is spotless with antiques and many flowers. A series of lounges and bars follow off to the right where guests tend to gather in a cozy setting. A large patio at the rear of the hotel is set with tables in nice weather and scans a majestic mountain panorama. On a lower level is a very large dining room dressed with light wooden furniture, light wooden beams with intricately carved supports, and enormous windows to soak in the view of the mountains. A small passageway left of the reception leads to the adjoining house which has been turned into part of the hotel. Cradles, old clocks, sleds, beautiful country peasant style chairs, tables and copper set a perfect mood. Our room was in another annex located just a half a block up the hill from the main hotel. Decorated simply the rooms are very pleasant and the views are dramatic. Our corner room, number 66, had a bay window enjoying a delightful panorama of the valley below.

HOTEL GUARDAVAL
Hotelier: Mr P.A. Regi
Address: CH-7550 Bad Scuol-Tarasp
Phone: (084) 9 13 21
Dates open: Dec-Apr and Jun-Oct
No. rooms: 48   *With shower/bath:* 36
Rates: Double with bath: Sfr 70-105
U.S.Representative: Romantik Hotels
Rep. Telephone No.: (800) 826-0015

For years I had heard of the wonderful Hotel Drei Konige - or the "Hotel of the Three Kings". Clients had raved about the wonderful setting directly on the banks of the Rhine, the impeccable service, wonderful food, and beautiful rooms. Although, it certainly cannot be classified as a cozy little inn, as I sat in my elegant room and gazed through the French windows watching the fascinating river traffic below, I knew that the Drei Konige must be included.

To quote from notes from the history of the oldest Swiss inn:
"The Three Kings Hotel in Basel, on the banks of the Rhine, has existed since 1026 and is thus by far the most ancient hostelry in Switzerland. This hotel has for centuries been in the leading rank, due to personalities who have visited it and because it has been one of the most frequented of all first-class hotels. Hotels such as these are part of the cultural and architectural heritage of old towns , just as much as are their ancient churches, town halls and guild houses. They are visited by makers of history and history is often made within their walls."

The Three Kings originally bore the name "Zur Blume", at the sign of the flower. But soon after the inn was founded, a historic meeting between three kings took place. The kings represented were: Conrade II, Emperor of the Holy Roman Empire; his son, (later known as Henry III) , and Rudolf III, the last King of Burgundy. At the meeting a treaty was drawn for the transferences of the territories which are now western Switzerland and southern France. The hotel's name was then changed, understandably, from "Zur Blume" to the Drei Konige. This old guest house is closely linked with world history and is often featured in literature. Many distinguished guests have frequented the inn, leaving their signatures in the golden guest book.

The Drei Konige is decorated with exquisite taste - formal antiques and lovely reproductions are in the public and guest rooms. Although, the rooms do vary they all maintain a delightful standard of decorating style. The bathrooms are generally large and equipped with many conveniences: enormous tubs, two wash stands, an automatic hair dryer, giant towels, a bidet and towel warmer. Rooms overlooking the Rhine warrant a splurge and the suites are spectacular , especially the Napoleon Suite, in regal shades of blue and an ornate ceiling - fit for a king!

HOTEL DREI KONIGE
Hotelier: Mr G. Ianna
Address: Blumenrain 8-10
          CH-4051 Basel
Phone: (061) 25 52 52   *Telex:* 629 37
Dates open: All Year
No. rooms: 82   *With shower/bath:* 82
Rates: Double with bath: Sfr 190-280;
Suites from Sfr 280-600
Credit cards: AX, DC, VS, CB, EC
U.S.Representative: H.R.I.
Rep. Telephone No.: (800) 223-6800

BERNE   *BELLEVUE PALACE*

Berne is a delightful city that draws many visitors, and without question, the Bellevue Palace, although not a little inn, is divine. The decorating throughout sets an atmosphere of elegant sophistication. It has a dignified, formal entrance in subdued colors. The dining room is gorgeous with rich wood paneling and tables set with crisp white linen, flowers and beautiful dinner ware. The lighting from wall sconces is soft and intimate. The bedrooms are spacious and tastefully decorated, individual in their style and color. The terrace at at the rear of the hotel is perhaps what impressed me most. The view from the terrace is beautiful and here the formal mood vanishes as guests gather in this charming rendezvous. The Hotel Bellevue Palace deserves every star in its deluxe rating.

BELLEVUE PALACE
Hotelier: Jacques A. Kuenzli
Address: Kochergasse 3-5
　　　　　 CH-3001 Berne
Phone: (031) 22 45 81　　　*Telex:* 321 24
Dates open: All Year
No. rooms: 150　　　*With shower/bath:* 150
Rates: Double with bath: Sfr 210-260
Credit cards: AE, VS, DC, MC, EC
U.S.Representative: L.R.I.
Rep. Telephone No.: (800) 232-2169

BUSINGEN, GERMANY　　*HOTEL ALTE RHEINMUHLE*

The Alte Rheinmuhle has such a spectacular setting and came so highly recommended, that although it is not in Switzerland, I decided to include it temporarily until my guide on the inns of Germany is published. To justify its inclusion, I rationalized that even though it is in a little niche of Germany, it is practically surrounded by Switzerland. And besides, I fell in love with the hotel and decided that I would improvise any excuse necessary to include it!

The Alte Rheinmuhle is only two and a half miles east of Schaffhausen. The distance is so short and the town so Swiss that customs are friendly and casual although you do need your passports to cross the border.

There is nothing more charming that an old mill converted to a hotel. The Alte Rheinmuhle is truly a wonderful transformation accomplished with delightful taste. Even if the decor were not perfection, the site itself would overcome many faults. The building dates from 1674 and sits right on the edge of the Rhine with the front of the hotel actually in the water. On the first floor is a beautiful dining room whose large windows overlook the Rhine. As you dine you can watch the constant boat traffic intermingled with the graceful slowly gliding swans. The hotel has earned an outstanding reputation for its cuisine and extensive wine cellar. Some of the restaurant's specialties include superb venison, wild rabbit and the highlight for dessert is the most scrumptious cassis sherbet to be found anywhere! I discussed the rooms with the management and was told that all rooms are all decorated in a country style and furnished with antiques - some even have four poster beds. Request a room facing the river. I cannot think of anything more romantic than a gourmet dinner in an enchanting restaurant, then climb the stairs to be lulled to sleep by the Rhine flowing beneath your window.

HOTEL ALTE RHEINMUHLE
Owner: Othmar Ernst
Manager: Alfred Wagner
Address: D-7701 Busingen
      GERMANY
Phone: (049) 07734/6076   *Telex:* 793 788
No. rooms: 15   *With shower/bath:* 12
Rates: DM 65-80
Credit cards: AE, DC

A sense of adventure and a glorious day tempted me away from the little town of Castagnola up the lakeside path toward the town of Gandria. I was not looking for a hotel, so if it had not been for the distracting smell of delicious freshly baked bread wafting across my path, I probably would never have discovered either the Hotel Elvezia al Lago nor the Fischer's Seehotel. However, the tempting fragrance of the bread baking in an outdoor oven of the lakeside cafe of the Hotel Elvezia was irresistable and I had to stop to investigate.

The *HOTEL AL LAGO* has a delightful outdoor terrace on the lake front. The hotel is across the walking path from the lake with an indoor cafe and a little bar. On the upper level are bedrooms - several with balconies providing delightful lake views.

The *FISCHER'S SEEHOTEL* is situated directly on the edge of Lake Lugano. There is a dining room marvelously situated overlooking the lake and a lounge area with "homey" Victorian decor.

Neither of these two hotels are deluxe, but both have great potential for the traveler on a budget. Their location is superb - directly on Lake Lugano with the only access by boat (the ferry dock is very convenient to both) or by the romantic foot path that hugs the lake front connecting the towns of Gandria and Castagnola. These two hotels are isolated from any city noises and couldn't offer a more tranquil atmosphere.

FISCHER'S SEEHOTEL HOTEL
Hotelier: Familie J. Fischer
Address: CH-6976 Castagnola
Phone: (091) 51 55 71
Dates open: March - October
No. rooms: 18
Rates: Double Sfr 60 - 80

ELVEZIA AL LAGO
Hotelier: Herbert Lucke
Address: CH-6976 Castagnola
Phone: (091) 51 44 51
Dates open: Jan 4 - Oct 24
No. rooms: 5 without bath
Rates: Double Sfr 50

60 **CHUR**   *HOTEL STERN*

Every aspect of the Hotel Stern has been designed and managed with the guest in mind. It might not be considered a glamorous hotel, yet it is obvious that behind every detail is someone who cares and works very hard to achieve the greatest comforts. Mr. Pfister, the owner, is a true professional in his field. He was away on business at the time of my arrival and so the supervision of the Stern became the sole responsibility of his wife. Mrs. Pfister told me that she is normally in charge of the bookkeeping and the hotel staff while her husband tends the front desk and the kitchen. She apologized saying it is her husband who is in public relations and she is mostly the "background". It was hard to imagine, however, how anyone could possibly be more charming, gentle and kind than Mrs. Pfister and I am certain the fact that the hotel runs so smoothly is a reflection of her own quiet, efficient manner.

Located in the old section of Chur, the Hotel Stern dates back three hundred years and is a wonderful blend of traditional decor enhanced by modern conveniences. In the twenty years that the Pfisters have owned the Hotel Stern they have been dedicated to providing choice accommodations and an excellent restaurant. They have done a tremendous job rebuilding and refurbishing the building. The furnishings are principally of the light Pine wood so typical in the Grison area of Switzerland. The decor also greatly profits from the fact that Mr. Pfister is an avid art collector and throughout the hotel are many skillfully displayed works of original art. There is a wonderful collection of the paintings of the famous Swiss artist, Mr. Carigiet, whose whimsical scenes are inspired by his own childhood in a small country village.

Another interesting collection of the Pfisters is a fabulous assortment of horse drawn carriages and sleds. The various buggies are stored in a garage behind the hotel. The collection, which is like a tiny museum, ranges from simple country sleds to gorgeous carriages fit for nobility. Mrs. Pfister had a cute story about her father-in-law whose love of the old horse drawn carriages and sleighs led to this fabulous collection. A few years ago when in his seventies, he agreed as a favor to a friend to drive one of the carriages all the way to Germany for a political celebration. Enroute he had an accident, was hospitalized, and ordered by the doctor to remain in bed and not continue the journey. Undaunted, the senior Mr. Pfister "escaped" the hospital, caught up with his carriage, and arrived on time in splendor and style! Any car buff would also envy a more modern counterpart, Mr. Pfister's 1932 Buick Sedan. With a brown exterior and dusty rose colored velvet interior, it is truly gorgeous and in mint condition. As the city fathers were opposed to the use of the horse and carriages on public roads, the Pfisters instead use the Buick on special occasions to pick up celebrities from the station.

HOTEL STERN
Hotelier: Mr. Emil Pfister
Address: Reichgasse 11
          CH-7000 Chur
Phone: (081) 22 35 55   *Telex:* 74198
Dates open: All Year
No. rooms: 55   *With shower/bath:* 55
Rates: Double room: Sfr 90-98
Credit cards: AE, VS, DC, MC, CB, EC
U.S.Representative: Romantik Hotels
Rep. Telephone No.: (800) 826-0015

 COPPET   *HOTEL DU LAC*

The Hotel du Lac is located only about six miles east of Geneva on the north shore of Lake Geneva in the town of Coppet. I had heard so much about the charm of the Hotel du Lac with its lovely lakeside setting that as we drove up I was quite disappointed. The hotel fronts directly onto a busy road and at first introduction it really does not appear to be a lake front hotel - much less a garden hotel. However through the lobby and a small and cozy lounge area, beyond to another lobby and, suddenly like magic the gardens and the lake could be seen from the exquisite dining room. The Proprietor, Rene Gottraux, is a famed chef, Officier -Rotisseur!

If you prefer simpler dining there is also the "Bistro" or in nice weather you can dine informally outside on the terrace. I enjoyed walking outside behind the hotel amongst the trees, green grass and a small garden leading down to the lakefront pier.

The Du Lac carries the air of an elegant home rather than that of a hotel. It also does not appear very old, but it is. In fact, in 1626 the Hotel Du Lac received the honor of enjoying *"the exclusive right to receive and lodge people arriving by coach or horseback."* At that time travelers by foot were excluded as guests of the inn because as a memorandum dated 1768 decreed " *there is too great a difference in men's conditions and fortunes ... the titled man of wealth riding in his own coach and four, attended by many servants must not be housed with the peasant, the labourer, the craftsman, the knife-sharperner, the chimney-sweep .. the latter would feel too ill at ease."*

The Hotel du Lac has been carefully restored and now you too can dream you are one of the guests arriving by *"coach and four"*. However there is no need to bring your own servants for when you arrive you will find the hotel's staff dutifully awaiting to attend to your every need. The hotel has retained many of its old beams, stone walls, and lovely antique furniture and artifacts. Most of the bedrooms have an "old world" feeling, but they are done in a combination of styles. Some have a Spanish flavor with large wooden headboards. My favorite rooms were done in a copy of French-antique. All the bedrooms are attractive; some have kitchenettes; some have balconies with views of the lake; some have a small terrace squeezed into the jumble of tile roof tops.

If you would prefer to be on the lakefront in a peaceful surrounding, but still be only a few miles away from the sophisticated city of Geneva, you might find the Hotel du Lac a perfect choice. It is very popular, so make a reservation far in advance.

HOTEL DU LAC
Hotelier: J & N Dallinges-Gottraux
Address: CH-1296 Coppet
Phone: (022) 76 15 21   *Telex:* 27639
Dates open: All Year
No. rooms: 16   *With shower/bath:* 16
Rates: Double room: Sfr 120-160,
        Apartments: Sfr 240-500
Credit cards: AE, VS, DC, EC
U.S.Representative: David B. Mitchell
Rep. Telephone No.: (415) 546-1311/SFO
            (212) 696-1323/NYC

 **CORSEREY**   *RELAIS DU VIEUX MOULIN*

Since I am a soft touch for any converted old mill, we made a special detour to inspect the Relais du Vieux Moulin. As soon as we drove up and saw the charming setting - nestled next to a little creek - and the attractive stucco and wood facade, I knew the detour was well worthwhile. Mrs. Elizabeth Brouwer, who owns and manages the inn, is most gracious, and emphasized that the inn is principally a restaurant rather than a hotel. The intimate, little dining room, radiating charm with its many antiques, would indeed make dining a pleasure. Glancing at the many awards on the wall we could further see that this was not just an ordinary restaurant, but rather a gourmet's delight and that a meal would be a memorable occasion.

Le Relais du Vieux Moulin has five bedrooms, all of which open onto one central lounge area located up a short flight of stairs from the entry. It is important to note that each room though very small, is tastefully decorated with furniture colorfully painted in a bright alpine motif. This dear little inn is ideal for those who love to dine, linger over coffee and then be only a few steps away from a comfortable bed and a good night's sleep.

RELAIS DU VIEUX MOULIN
Hotelier: Elizabeth Brouwer
Address: CH-1751 Corserey
Phone: (037) 30 14 44
No. rooms: 5 / None with private bath
Rates: Double room: Sfr 80
Credit cards: AE, DC, VS, EC

 **CULLY**   *AUBERGE DU RAISIN*

The Auberge du Raisin is located in a small village on Lake Geneva. The hotel itself is about a block from Lake Geneva near a little park fronting the lake. Cully nestles in a marvelous section of Switzerland - especially when the vineyards draping the steep slopes of the north shore of Lake Geneva announce the harvest in their new fall colors.

Like many hotels in this guide, the fame of Auberge du Raisin is based on its reputation for excellent food and wines. The outside of the hotel appears rather ordinary, however once inside the feeling changes to one of warmth and friendliness. Although the exterior of the Auberge does not exude the feeling of antiquity, it does actually date back to the year 1500!

I was not able to see any of the rooms since every room was occupied and in proper Swiss consideration, the manager did not want to invade their guests' privacy. However, while at dinner in Saas Fee a few nights later I was sharing travel experiences with other guests at our table who had been at the Auberge du Raisin the night before. They loved the hotel reaffirming the dining as "exquisite" and also said the bedrooms were very pleasant although simply decorated.

AUBERGE DU RAISIN
Hotelier: Mr A. Blokbergen
Address: CH-1096 Cully
Phone: (021) 99 21 31
Dates open: All Year
No. rooms: 13
Rates: Double room : Sfr 105 - 120
Credit cards: AE, DC, VS, EC

 **GENEVA** *LE RICHEMOND*

Having visited Le Richemond on previous trips to Geneva, I remembered it as being my favorite of the more formal lakeside hotels. This time again, of the majestic queens which nestle around the right bank of Lake Geneva, Le

Richemond is the winner! Actually, it is not directly situated on the lake, but rather, faces a small park about a half a block away. It still enjoys lake views across the park, but has an advantage in being off the noisy main street.

Having one hundred rooms, Le Richemond is small for a city hotel and has a very warm and inviting air. There is a garden restaurant as you enter and on the left, a cozy bar with dark wood paneling. A marvelous dining room sits further back with dark walls and fresh flowers on all the intimate dining tables.

Although not a country inn, for a charming hotel with a definite "olde worlde" flavor and a prime location in Geneva, you will be pleased with Le Richemond.

LE RICHEMOND
Owner: J. Armleder
Manager: R. Klinger
Address: Jardin Brunswick
           CH-1201 Geneva
Phone: (022) 31 14 00   *Telex:* 22598
Dates open: All Year
No. rooms: 150
Rates: Double room: Sfr 250-300
Credit cards: AE, VS, DC, EC
U.S.Representative: H.R.I.
Rep. Telephone No.: (800) 223-6800

Geneva is known for its lovely lakeside hotels, but my heart in any city gravitates toward the oldest section where you can wander from your hotel back several centuries and relive the magic of bygone ages. On previous visits I've always searched the twisting little streets of the old town looking for a wonderful small hotel, but without success. This time I had heard of a newly opened hotel in the 'vielle ville' so eagerly I made a reservation. When I walked into a cozy, intimate lobby and met a warm welcome from the concierge, I knew I would not be disappointed. There was no sign of any tour groups only the presence of other guests sitting in a small lounge, talking quietly or reading; using the hotel as they would their home.

My room, number 202, had a queen-sized bed, a small round table accompanied by antique style high backed arm chairs, bedside tables with lamps, a small refrigerator and a very nice bathroom with a permanently installed hair dryer. The room was quite small but very cozy with beamed ceiling and wood-paned windows looking over a quiet shaded square and an old fountain. I loved it. Unable to visit all the rooms as the hotel was almost full, I was quite pleased with the few that I saw. Room 201 was similar to ours, but with twin beds. The junior suites afford a little more room, as they are bedrooms with a sitting area. When making a reservation, I would definitely request a room overlooking the square.

Hotel Les Armures is difficult to find. The 'vielle ville' of Geneva climbs steeply up the hillside, above the left bank of the river. Most of the streets are closed to traffic, making access a bit more complicated. However, Les Armures' neighbor is the majestic St. Peter's Cathedral and its soaring spires are easy to see. Watch for St. Peter's and the prediction is that you will find a treasure at the end of your hunt!

HOTEL LES ARMURES
Owner: Amadee Granges
Manager: Hubert Escher
Address: 1 Rue du Puits St Pierre
            CH-1204 Geneva
Phone: (022) 28 91 72   *Telex:* 421129
Dates open: All Year
No. rooms: 28   *With shower/bath:* 28
Rates: Double room: Sfr 200-260
Credit cards: AE, DC, EC, MC

 GLION   *HOTEL VICTORIA*

The Hotel Victoria enjoys a prime location in a parklike setting in the suburb of Montreux called Glion, perched in the hills above the city. With the sun out on a balmy June day, we walked through the gorgeous grounds with guests everywhere savoring the beautiful view over Lake Geneva.

Inside, the first impression of the hotel is set by a rather dark and formal reception area. However, as you continue the hotel opens onto some charming public rooms. There is also a cheerful, bright, garden "sun room"; a delightful spot to enjoy a good book or afternoon tea. The bar area is cozy with dark paneling enhanced by old world paintings, and there are two delightful and beautifully decorated dining rooms. The cuisine is delicious and the manager, Mr. Mittemair, is like a host in a private home. He mingled throughout the dining room at dinner time, to observe that all his guests were cared for and happy. His graciousness and warmth served to soften the formal atmosphere of the hotel.

We settled into a spectacular room, decorated with fine antique reproductions and a glorious view which stretched across the town of Montreux, over the lake, to the mountains beyond. Sunset painted our view with soft pastels, the picture changed to one of twinkling lights as dusk turned into night. We ate breakfast outside on our balcony, again enjoying the view - this time misty in the early breath of dawn.

When renovations are completed, all the rooms will be similar in style and decor to the one we occupied. However, until then, some of the rooms are a bit dark and stuffy. It is well worth the additional cost to reserve a room that overlooks the lake. I only hope you will be blessed with the magic of fine weather to highlight the views and enhance the memories of your stay.

HOTEL VICTORIA
Hotelier: Toni Mittermair
Address: CH-1823 Glion
Phone: (021) 63 31 31   *Telex:* 453 102
Dates open: All Year
No. rooms: 40   *With shower/bath:* 35
Rates: Sfr 125-170

This hotel is a conglomerate of buildings of various styles, but all with a truly spectacular location. One portion, an intricately timbered building, practically sits in the Rhine River flowing in front of the hotel. A wonderful patio, banked with bright red geraniums, extends out over the water similar to a boat deck. As the hotel extends back from the river, it becomes a delightful mixture of nooks and crannies, turrets and gables. Another portion of the hotel, although less of a "gingerbread type", is equally charming. The restaurant of the Hotel Drachenburg is famous for its delicious trout, caught fresh from the Rhine.

The Hotel Drachenburg and Waaghaus is included practically on the merit of its location alone. At the time of my visit the hotel was completed reserved, so I was unable to see any of the bed rooms. The receptionist informed me that there are plans to renovate and redecorate all the bedrooms in this next year. However, the setting of this hotel is so beautiful and tranquil that, no matter how the rooms are decorated, the hotel promises a memorable stay.

HOTEL DRACHENBURG AND WAAGHAUS
Hotelier: Familie Martin-Hummel
Address: CH-8274 Gottlieben
Phone: (072) 69 14 14
No. rooms: 54
Rates: Double room: Sfr 120-140

With the Rhine directly in front narrowing to connect with Lake Constance, the setting of the Hotel Krone is truly idyllic. An intimate terrace occupies the water's edge and in good weather is set with an inviting cluster of dining tables. Characteristic of so many Swiss inns, inside the decorating focus seems to be on the dining facilities and the accommodations take second priority. The ambiance of the dining room is delightful; fresh flowers are lavishly used and the paneling and furnishings are beautiful. The rooms, with the exception of two facing the river that are in a style representative of when Napoleon frequented this region, are quite simple in their decor. However, what difference does it make if the bedrooms or reception hall are not candidates for "Architectural Digest" when the food is so outstanding, and the service so superb?

HOTEL KRONE
Hotelier: George Schraner-Michaeli
Address: CH-8274 Gottlieben
Phone: (072) 69 23 23
Dates open: All Year
No. rooms: 23   *With shower/bath:* 23
Rates: Double room: Sfr 90-200
Credit cards: AE, DC, VS, EC
U.S.Representative: Romantik Hotels
Rep. Telephone No.: (800) 826-0015

Sometimes I will include a town because of an inn's location, but in this case, I've included an inn because I fell in love with the town. The mountain village of Grimentz is a bundle of old, storybook, darkened wood timbered chalets, brilliantly accented with colorful flowers. This village deserves to be explored and its appeal demands that you linger. Tucked at the entrance to the village is a pretty little inn, white washed with handsome wood shutters and an owner whose hospitality rivals the charm of the town. The Hotel de Moiry has a few, very simple but welcome rooms allowing the opportunity to spend the night in Grimentz. Number eleven is the nicest room. Found on the top floor, it has its own private bath and windows that open up onto the most refreshing mountain vistas. Marvelous sunshine blessed our visit and we were able to dine on the patio in front of the hotel enjoying a memorable meal of fondue, salad, crusty, dark bread and beer. The dining room inside is warmed by a cozy fireplace, and the tables are set with fresh cloths and flowers. Be sure to seek out a striking wall mural that depicts both a tradition of the valley and a justified pride of the management - this mural is a portrayal of an annual competition between the cows of the area to determine the leader. Those of the Hotel de Moiry are consistently the winners and recognized as the strongest!

HOTEL DU MOIRY
Hotelier: Vital Salamin
Address: CH-3961 Grimentz
Phone: (027) 65 11 41
Dates open: All Year
No. rooms: 35
Rates: Sfr 42-64

As you drive into Grindelwald a small church with its clock tower and high peaked steeple rises dramatically against the mountain backdrop. Just beyond this little church is a parking area with a spectacular view of the fabulous alpine range. After soaking in this view my attention was drawn to a small shuttered hotel across the street. I entered the Fiescherblick and felt very fortunate to find the owner, Mr. Brawand-Hauser tending the reception area. The hotel is not fancy but does possess a most inviting atmosphere. As you enter the lobby the feeling is set by a great old Swiss clock, a painted Swiss wall cupboard, a little table joined by a regional alpine chair and a few very old milking stools. The dining room is decorated with modern furniture but the flowers on the tables, and the pewter mugs and antiques that adorn the walls add warmth to the area. In addition to the main room, there is an outdoor restaurant at street level and an even more dramatic little terrace set with tables one level up. Mr Brawand-Hauser personally offered a guided tour of the hotel. I was intrigued with the many little niches artistically displaying antique farm implements. Mr Brawand explained that the inn was originally his family's home and the collection of various farm tools were used on his father's farm. In one area are a number of cheese making utensils, churns, a milking stool, the sieves and the wooden frames. Upstairs the old world feeling vanishes, but the rooms are clean and tidy. Some of the bedrooms have a small balcony and the views are so startling that the simplicity of the rooms by contrast, seems only appropriate.

HOTEL FIESCHERBLICK
Hotelier: Mr Johannes Brawand
Address: CH-3818 Grindelwald
Phone: (036) 53 11 64
Dates open: May/Oct and Dec/Apr
No. rooms: 23   *With shower/bath:* 23
Rates: Double room: Sfr 92-124 on a
        demi-pension basis
Credit cards: VS, DC, EC, MC

 GRUYERES   *HOTEL DES CHEVALIERS*

The Hotel des Chevaliers is very well known as a popular base for visiting the wonderful hilltop, medieval village of Gruyeres. The hotel is located on a rise above the main parking lot of the village and very easy to find. A wonderful patio outside with white lawn chairs is constantly occupied by guests soaking up the stupendous view. It was not surprising to find the Hotel Des Chevaliers full on the occasion of both my visits. However, I donned my Sherlock cap and was able to peer into a number of the rooms to investigate the type of accommodations! The bedrooms are found in one building with a small reception desk on the lower level. The bedrooms have a country feeling because of the simplicity of the furniture against the white, freshly painted walls, and I was intrigued by the gorgeous, unobstructed views that the bedrooms at the back would have over the rolling hills and up to the high mountains. Even more captivating is the charm of a second building housing a collection of little rooms for dining: the Salle des

Chevaliers, the Chambre Gruyerienne, and the Jardin d'Hiver - each one having captured a feeling of warmth and welcome. Country antiques fill the rooms; copper hangings and country, blue and white tiles adorn the walls; the floors are laid in handsome tiles; masses of beautiful flower arrangements are found everywhere, and the soft and constant ticking of an old grandfather clock escapes from one of the dining rooms setting quite a romantic mood.

Return to Gruyeres and the Hotel des Chevaliers as it is definitely part of the town's enchantment.

HOTEL DES CHEVALIERS
Owner: Mr Antoine Corboz
Hotelier: G. & S. Bouchery
Address: CH-1663 Gruyeres
Phone: (029) 6 19 33
Dates open: February to January
No. rooms: 34 *With shower/bath:* 34
Rates: Double room: Sfr 100-140
Credit cards: AE, VS, DC, EC

The Hostellerie de St Georges is a simple hotel ideally located at the heart of the marvelous little medieval village of Gruyeres. The hotel is named for old St George himself, and you will see our mighty hero slaying the dragon on the brightly colored emblem proudly displayed over the front door and again on a carving hung over an antique chest in the main hallway. Each bedroom is not only numbered, but also has a motif from the era of St George. As an example, on the door of one room there is a whimsical knight with a sword raised high, on another a musician playing an instrument similar to a bagpipe, while yet another has a witch-like character riding a broom. Each bedroom is similar in size and decor. If you book early you can have the great bonus of reserving a room with a view over the glorious, green pastured valley spotted with sleepy, grazing cattle. In winter the green pastures change to a blanket of white while the backdrop of mountains remains constant and dramatic all year.

Although the bedrooms are simple the dining room is very attractive and food cannot be categorized as anything but superb. We also soon discovered that those apparently lazy cattle were responsible for some of the most delicious cream and cheeses. Gruyeres cheese, famous the world over, is served at every meal and the Gruyeres cheese quiche of the hotel is so incomparably light and with such a delicate pastry, that it is tempting to order it at every meal. Our visit fortunately coincided with strawberry season, and so our dinner concluded with a large bowl of fruit smothered in the thickest cream I had ever seen! The fear of calories could not possibly compete with this truly sinful dessert!

Antiques are scattered throughout the public rooms and a small tricycle and baby buggy tucked under the hall stairway hint at the presence, personality and charm of the owner and his family. We were able to sample true hospitality the morning of our departure. We were downstairs well before the established breakfast hour, and yet Mr. Miedler was there to greet us. When he saw we were hoping for a bite to eat, without a moment's hesitation, he commissioned one of the waitresses to set out for the nearest bakery to fetch a basket of fresh rolls, and assigned another waitress the task of grinding and brewing some fresh coffee. It was his intention to see that every effort was made to make our stay enjoyable. We ate the delicious pastries in a small breakfast room which later in the day serves as the bar and lounge, and as the hour was yet early, we watched the school children bundled up and trudging off to school burdened with school books and satchels. Each child was also carrying a bouquet of flowers, and I pondered whether there was a special occasion or if this was a daily ritual. Either way, on that particular morning it left a sense of gaiety in the air. When the weather is warm enough, tables are set up in front of the hotel under an orange awning where the activity of the town is displayed before you, or better yet, tables are set out on the rear porch and the view opens up onto a lovely panorama of green pastures and the mountains beyond.

HOSTELLERIE DE ST. GEORGES
Hotelier: Mr Heribert Miedler
Address: CH-1663 Gruyeres
Phone: (029) 6 22 46
Dates open: March - November
No. rooms: 15
Rates: Double room: Sfr 80-120
Credit cards: AE, VS, DC, MC

The Hotel Olden was introduced to us by our Swiss friend, Dr Jean Carle. He and his charming wife, Idly, are residents of Gstaad and they are personally familiar with every hotel and restaurant in the vicinity. Knowing we were looking for small hotels with atmosphere and charm, Dr. Carle said we certainly must investigate the Hotel Olden. Our research discovered that indeed the Hotel Olden is quite famous. There are three restaurants in the hotel so well known that visiting dignitaries and movie stars frequent them when in Gstaad. The restaurant situation at the Hotel Olden is quite unique because under one roof gather all the local farmers and workmen who come to the old pub, "Pinte", and also the jet-set of the world who come to dine and dance in the other very chic restaurants. The menu is superb and includes a few favorites such as Fondue Chinoise which is a delicious fondue made with a bouillon base instead of with an oil base, and for dessert Gletscherkuss which is a scrumptious combination of vanilla ice cream and cherries flambe. The outside of the Hotel Olden is of a chalet style with cream colored facade and green shutters and of course in summer the ever present colorful flower boxes. In addition there are regional Bernese designs painted on the front of the building to accentuate the windows. An outdoor cafe is available to soak up the sun while dining.

The bedrooms are small and very simple, but they do have an extremely personal touch in that much of the furniture and walls have been painted delicately by the owner, Heidi Donizetti-Mulener, in the typical Swiss country designs.

Even if you do not stay at the Hotel Olden while in Gstaad, be sure to stop by for a meal and look around. Who knows, at the next table might be Audrey Hepburn or Richard Burton!

HOTEL OLDEN
Hotelier: Heidi Donizetti
Address: CH-3780 Gstaad
Phone: (030) 4 34 44
Dates open: All Year
No. rooms: 16   *With shower/bath:* 16
Rates: Double room: Sfr 120-200
Credit cards: AE, VS, DC, EC

 GSTAAD   *POST HOTEL ROSSLI*

Gstaad is one of Switzerland's most popular mountain retreats and the Post Rossli is an excellent hotel choice. Little touches show a special personal touch. There are plants in the entry and a few well placed antiques to give an inviting welcome, and off the hall are two marvelous dining rooms. One tends to be used for casual lunch hour. The other is truly charming with wood paneling, alpine style chairs carved with heart designs and tied merrily with red cushions, green plants, some old prints, and copper pieces displayed on the walls. Like the decor, the cuisine is exceptional. The bedrooms are pleasant, very comfortable but not outstanding in decor. However, they are all immaculately clean and on the beds are the wonderful fluffy down comforters which add such a fresh and cozy look to a room. Some of the rooms have their own balcony or porch, but since the hotel is located in the center of town the views are not spectacular. Gstaad is really quite a little city, but the country village aspect has not gone as we discovered upon awaking to the sound of melodic cow bells instead of the noise of traffic and looked out the window to see a herd of cows whose pace was governed by the sing-song chant of a young boy!

The underlying reason for the success and popularity of Hotel Post Rossli is the owner himself. Mr Widmer's presence is quite evident. He is available to welcome his guests, supervises the service in the dining room and conscientiously oversees every detail of operation. Suited to this mountain resort, Mr Widmer is young and ruggedly attractive; a mountaineer, who acts as a trail guide in the summer and ski guide during the winter months.

POST HOTEL ROSSLI
Hotelier: Mr Ruedi Widmer
Address: CH-3780 Gstaad
Phone: (030) 4 34 12
Dates open: Jun/Nov and Dec/Apr
No. rooms: 26 *With shower/bath:* 16
Rates: Double room with bath: Sfr 80-140
Credit cards: VS, DC, EC, MC

 **GSTEIG-GSTAAD** *HOTEL BAREN*

We were exploring the valley beyond Gstaad heading towards the southern mountain glaciers when we discovered the picture book hamlet of Gsteig. In the middle of the village near the church was one of the most engaging buildings we had come across in our meanderings, and we had seen to date many truly outstanding facades. The Hotel Baren is what is termed a typical Saanen-style house and this original seventeenth century wooden inn is such an outstanding specimen it is protected under special Swiss law. The hotel is actually owned by the town and the manager is hired by the village. The heavy, sculptured beams and intricately carved exterior walls are exquisite. In summer the cheerful geraniums at each window, red checked curtains peeking through the small window panes, plus the jaunty Swiss flags hanging from the upper windows enhance the image of the perfect Swiss inn. The decor in the dining room continues with the regional flavor. This cozy room is richly paneled and furnished with country style wooden chairs and tables. Red checked table cloths and fresh flowers on the tables add further charm. The inn is largely famous for its cuisine. However, there are several very simple, moderately decorated bedrooms whose beds are decked with inviting traditional soft, down comforters! Please note only one room has a private bathroom.

HOTEL BAREN
Address: CH-3781 Gsteig
Phone: (030) 51 033
Dates open: All Year
No. rooms: 7
Rates: Double room: Sfr 50-70

Clinging to a narrow shelf the old town of Guarda seems to precariously reach out over the Unter-Engadin valley. Gloriously sunny and warm, it was day of autumn perfection as we entered this town of twisting streets, characteristic old homes colored with flower boxes at every window, intricately carved old hay barns and spectacular views. Influenced by this absolutely magnificent day I was in the mood to find a gem of a hotel to match the charm of the village.

Almost the first hotel I saw was the Hotel Meisser, beautifully situated on a promontory overlooking the expanse of green valley below. On the lawn were tables set in the warm sunshine while waitresses in bright Alpine costumes were busy serving the happy guests. I could not have imagined a more blissful scene. Although the hotel does not appear to be extremely old, it does have some antiques used throughout the public areas and pieces of old copper, baskets of flowers, and heavy chests to add further cozy touches. The dining room, too, is most attractive. The accommodations are simple in their decor, fresh and clean, and best of all afford those who seek a region of spectacular beauty, a comfortable place to linger.

HOTEL MEISSER
Hotelier: Mr Ralf Meisser
Address: CH-7549 Guarda
Phone: (084) 9 21 32   *Telex:* 74637
Dates open: June to November
No. rooms: 25
Rates: Double room with bath: Sfr 64-72
    demi-pension rates, per person
Credit cards: DC, AE, VS

It was late afternoon as we drove into the hills south of Lucerne in search of the Hotel Waldhaus. As we passed by Lucerne we encountered the late afternoon traffic of a big city. After being in the countryside of Switzerland for several weeks, we longed to leave the cars and noise and return to peace and quiet. Therefore, we were very pleased to find that Horw, although only a short distance in miles, is far removed in mood from the city of Lucerne. The Hotel Waldhaus is situated in the gentle hills above Horw.

The Waldhaus definitely resembles a country manor. The present owners' love of horses is apparent throughout the hotel. As we climbed the stairs to our room there were striking prints of numerous racehorses; from our room looking out to the terrace we observed a number of guests lounging in their jodhpurs enjoying drinks, the late afternoon sun; and the sound of horses returning to their stables broke the countryside silence. We couldn't help but feel as if we had just arrived at an elegant estate and joined a private house party.

Dining was also very reminiscent of being in a private home. There is not one room but several formal, elegant, intimate dining areas each with windows looking out across the patio and beyond to a wide expanse of countryside vistas. The menu is exceptional, the meal delicious and served with professional grace and style.

If you desire a location convenient to Lucerne with the delightful quiet of the countryside, the Hotel Waldhaus will prove an excellent choice.

HOTEL WALDHAUS
Hotelier: Mr Kurt Buholzer
Address: CH-6048 Horw
Phone: (041) 47 17 54
Dates open: All Year
No. rooms: 18   *With shower/bath:* 18
Rates: Double room: Sfr 125-150
Credit cards: AE, DC, VS, EC
U.S.Representative: David B. Mitchell
Rep. Telephone No.: (415) 546-1311/SFO
                    (212) 696-1323/NYC

 INTERLAKEN   *HOTEL DU LAC*

The Hotel du Lac has a superb location directly on the banks of the Aare River as it flows between the two lakes of Brienz and Thun. Many of the bedrooms overlook the river and the guests awaken to enchanting river views, to a peaceful scene of boats and swans gliding below the window. Pink with a French mansard roof, the Hotel du Lac has about fifty rooms. All of the bedrooms are simple in their furnishings, however, the superior rooms with views of the river and boat traffic are well worth the additional cost. Paneled in wood the lobby is cozy, informal and has a number of corner hideaways. For dining there are two rooms. One is in a new addition, quite attractive with large windows that open onto lovely river views, while the second less formal dining room is decorated with wooden tables, chairs and brightly colored table cloths.

If you come to the Hotel du Lac expecting a charming little country inn, you will be disappointed. If you come to the Hotel du Lac expecting a small, older hotel with antiquated charm, adequate accommodations, and a location which couldn't be more convenient for a Jungfrau excursion, you should be very content here.

HOTEL DU LAC
Hotelier: Mr Peter Hofmann
Address: Hoheweg 225
　　　　　CH-3800 Interlaken
Phone: (036) 22 29 22　　　*Telex:* 923 100
Dates open: All Year
No. rooms: 45
Rates: Double room: Sfr 46-86
Credit cards: AE, VS, MC,
U.S.Representative: Best Western
Rep. Telephone No.: (800) 528-1234

 **INTERLAKEN** *HOTEL VICTORIA JUNGFRAU*

The grandeur of the Victoria Jungfrau is famous throughout the world. Mr Edouard Ruchti, a member of the Swiss Federal Parliament, commissioned the building of the hotel in 1864, and it's exclusive design was dictated by the clientele he intended to attract. Although it was hopeful that Queen Victoria might one day grace the guest list, reflected in the hotel's name, she never managed a trip to Interlaken.

Perfected over a span of one hundred years, the Victoria Jungfrau is considered one of Switzerland's most deluxe hotels and the service is refined and faultless. Elegance captivates the atmosphere. The accommodations are spacious, many with large balconies. The sporting facilities offered by the hotel - an indoor swimming pool as well as indoor and outdoor tennis courts - are in keeping with, and complement the resort setting. The hotel opens on to grazing grounds, prohibited from development by the town. Across this park-like pasture guests can absorb some of the regions most spectacular mountain vistas.

Stay here, enjoy the luxury of the facilities, be pampered by the service, and pretend, that you are perhaps, one of the royalty for whom Mr Ruchti built the hotel.

HOTEL VICTORIA JUNGFRAU
Hotelier: Emanuel Berger
Address: Hoheweg 41
         CH-3800 Interlaken
Phone: (036) 21 21 71   *Telex:* 923 121
Dates open: mid-December to end-October
No. rooms: 220   *With shower/bath:* 220
Rates: Double room: Sfr 230-290;
      Suites: Sfr 600-1000
Credit cards: AE, VS, DC, MC
U.S.Representative: H.R.I.
Rep. Telephone No.: (800) 223-6800

The Royal Hotel Bellevue is one of the fanciest hotels in this guide. It is much more sophisticated in the amenities it has to offer than most of the other inns ... there are tennis courts, a beautiful outdoor pool, a second elaborate indoor pool, sauna, and even horseback riding (riding clothes are desirable, boots obligatory) . It is included not because of all the extra niceties offered, but rather because of the hotel's fantastic location at the end of the beautiful Kandertal valley. The road ends in Kandersteg. If you want to continue over the mountains beyond Kandersteg on the "short cut" to the Rhone Valley, you must put your car on the piggy back train which will take you through the tunnel to Brig. Kandersteg is absolutely beautiful with the mountains rising in a semi-circle around the little town. The front of the Royal Hotel Bellevue faces the road, but the rear of the hotel opens up in a splendid vista across gorgeous meadows to the mountain peaks. The back lawn of the hotel in summer is a velvet carpet of grass with an outdoor pool surrounded by comfortable lounges.

The interior of the Royal Hotel Bellevue, although only recently constructed, reflects an old world elegance with oriental rugs, cavernous fireplaces, comfy leather sofas, tapestries on the wall, and some antiques scattered about to accentuate the traditional ambiance. The dining room is especially beautiful with intricately designed paneled ceiling, giant chandeliers, upholstered arm chairs, and tables set with crisp white table cloths and candles. The bedrooms vary tremendously in their color schemes. Some of the bedrooms for my taste were a little overdone with ornate furniture, velvets, and brocades. The bedrooms I preferred were decorated with simpler furnishings. The views from the bedrooms are so lovely that it is impossible for man to compete with the decoration that nature provides out each window.

ROYAL HOTEL BELLEVUE
Hotelier: Familie A. Rikli
Address: CH-3718 Kandersteg
Phone: (033) 75 12 12   *Telex:* 922 192
Dates open: December to October
No. rooms: 30   *With shower/bath:* 30
Rates: Double room: Sfr 80-180
Credit cards: AE, EC, VS
U.S.Representative: David B. Mitchell
Rep. Telephone No.: (415) 546-1311/SFO
              (212) 696-1323/NYC

 KLEINE SCHEIDEGG   *KLEINE SCHEIDEGG HOTEL*

Almost considered a landmark of Switzerland, the Kleine Scheidegg Hotel sits on a barren, windswept landscape that challenges all but the giant Eiger. It is recognized by many for its part in the staging of the adventure movie, "The Eiger Sanction". At the time of our visit the rooms were all reserved, and so unfortunately it was not possible to stay at the hotel. When I attempted to question the receptionist about the accommodations and their decor, I was told in a very matter of fact manner, "that of course they are lovely, if the rooms were not nice why else would the hotel always be full and people return year after year? ". If not an informative description, it does seem a logical answer!

The town of Kleine Scheidegg consists of just a few sparsely scattered buildings serving as the junction for trains from Grindelwald and Lauterbrunnen bound for the Jungfraujoch.

KLEINE SCHEIDEGG HOTEL
Hotelier: Frau Heidi von Almen
Address: CH-3801 Kleine Scheidegg
Phone: (036) 55 12 12   *Telex:* 923 235
Dates open: Jun/Sept & Dec/May
No. rooms: 60
Rates: Sfr 155-200

KLOSTERS   *HOTEL CHESA GRISHUNA*

It had been twelve years since I had visited the Chesa Grishuna, but the memories of that visit lingered with such vivid pleasure that I knew if the hotel still existed I would want to include it in this guide. I only hoped that my memories would not overwhelm my objectivity.

So visit the Chesa Grishuna I did; traveling the same, short walk from the train station. The season was different, the cozy blanket of snow of winter having turned with spring into clusters of brightly colored flowers but the interior was as I remembered , romantic and cozy. If anything, time has been extremely kind with the inn appearing even more charming than the visions of my memory. We were first here on a ski holiday, and the warmth of the Chesa Grishuna was one of the few temptations to succeed in getting us off the slope. Warm weathered paneling enriches most of the public rooms, antique furnishings, and accents of copper pieces and artistic flower arrangements blend beautifully. Without the benefit of antiques, the bedrooms achieve the country feeling with the use of charming provincial wallpapers and matching fabrics, copies of traditional swiss furniture, exposed beams and the character of gently, sloping floors. Some of the bedrooms are a bit cozy and small, but all nicely done and if you are on a budget you might want to consider a room without bath.

The dining room is exceptional in cuisine, service and "country formal" atmosphere. The personality of the staff matches the character and charm of the inn. While here on our skiing holiday, Michael, who was then only thirteen, could never decide on an his main course. Each evening the menu was set before him, and each evening the waiter stood patiently by, awaiting his decision. It was perhaps our fourth night, and when again, that night Michael could not seem to decide what to order, the waiter disappeared. I guessed and sympathetically understood that he had come to the end of his patience. My assumptions were proved wrong as he instead consulted with the maitre d'. In a few minutes that wonderful man, who knew the mystique of little boys, returned and held out two straws. "Choose one", he challenged. And when Michael showed him the straw, the maitre d' with a twinkle in his eye said, "How lucky you are, you have just won the roast beef!"

The Chesa Grishuna will always remain one of my favorite Swiss inns. I thank them for the quality of accommodations, service and the cherished memories.

HOTEL CHESA GRISHUNA
Hotelier: Hans & Christian Guler
Address: CH-7250 Klosters
Phone: (083) 4 22 22   *Telex:* 74248
Dates open: All Year
No. rooms: 33   *With shower/bath:* 19
Rates: Double room with bath: Sfr 230-
       310 on a demi-pension basis
Credit cards: AE, VS, DC
U.S.Representative: Romantik Hotels
Rep. Telephone No.: (800) 826-0015

 KUSSNACHT AM RIGI   *HOTEL DU LAC SEEHOF*

The Hotel du Lac Seehof is located on Lake Lucerne at Kussnacht. Many steamers that ply the lake stop here, and as the hotel is ideally situated directly on the water front where the boats dock, it serves as a popular luncheon spot. The town of Kussnacht is rather noisy and bustling with tourists, but you have a feeling of tranquillity in the oasis of the hotel's garden terrace restaurant. The Hotel du Lac Seehof has been in the Trutmann family for five generations and is now managed by Albert Trutmann and his attractive wife, Joan. Albert Trutmann lived in the United States for a number of years and speaks perfect English and understands American tastes.

The Trutmanns at the time of my visit were in the process of refurbishing the inn.

Downstairs, the dining room to the left of the front hall is delightfully decorated with antiques. It is elegant but not pretentious, and very inviting. Mr Trutmann showed me the bedrooms which have been redecorated. They are all without private bath, but are pleasant and spacious.

I recommend this hotel as a fun stopover when on a lake excursion, especially, if you want to linger over dinner and do not mind sharing a bathroom. I imagine by the time you arrive the hotel will have improved immensely as the Trutmanns are young, enthusiastic, the perfect hosts and constantly making improvements.

HOTEL DU LAC SEEHOF
Hotelier: A. Trutmann
Address: CH-6403 Kussnacht am Rigi
Phone: (041) 81 10 12
Dates open: All Year
No. rooms: 15 none with private bath
Rates: Double room: Sfr 55-60

KUSSNACHT AM RIGI   *GASTHAUS ENGEL*

Kussnacht is a main stop for the ferry boats which ply Lake Lucerne. Should you want to overnight here you would enjoy the Gasthaus Engel. The oldest part of the building dates back to 1405. In 1552 a second section to the building was constructed and from that period its appearance has remained unchanged for over four hundred years. The atmosphere of the hotel is established by the cream colored facade textured with a cross work of old beams and green shutters. The charm of the outside is reinforced inside. The dining room is ornately paneled in walnut, which interestingly enough came from one tree, also centuries old. The tables are laid out with cheerful country checked cloths. The guest rooms at the Gasthaus Engel vary tremendously. Some are extremely plain with modern decor, others have gorgeous old wood paneling and antique furniture.

GASTHAUS ENGEL
Hotelier: Hans Ulrich
Address: CH-6403 Kussnacht am Rigi
Phone: (041) 81 10 57
Dates open: All Year
No. rooms: 12
Rates: Double room: Sfr 78-105

 **LUCERNE**   *HOTEL CHATEAU GUTSCH*

On a gloriously sunny day I rode the tram to the top of the hillside to further investigate the Hotel Chateau Gutsch. Settling on the hotel's terrace I was captivated by the panorama of Lucerne stretching before me. My impression of the hotel on an earlier visit had been that it was a bit too dramatic and ornately decorated to include in a book of country inns, however the day and the view erased any previous reservations.

Turrets, balconies and terraces dress the Chateau Gutsch in almost a fairytale atmosphere. When traveling with children the hotel's large swimming pool and wooded grounds, great for exploring, might prove an added bonus and a welcome respite from sightseeing and long drives. The dining room enjoys a country ambiance with wooden tables and chairs, large wine casks and warmed by an enormous fireplace. The menu has been under the excellent supervision of the same person for twenty years, the father of the assistant manager of the Wilden Mann Hotel.

One of my favorite hotels in Lucerne is the Wilden Mann. The Chateau Gutsch and the Wilden Mann are both owned by the Furler Family. The Wilden Mann had been in the Furler family for many years, while the Chateau Gutsch was owned by Mrs. Furler's family and was given to their daughter as a wedding present. Mr. and Mrs. Furler are both very active in running their hotels, working together they gracefully add style and perfection to the hotel business.

HOTEL CHATEAU GUTSCH
Owner: Mr & Mrs F.M. Furler
Manager: Mr & Mrs P.C. Wallimann
Address: Kanonenstrasse
       CH-6003 Lucerne
Phone: (041) 22 02 72   *Telex:* 72455
Dates open: All Year
No. rooms: 40   *With shower/bath:* 40
Rates: Double room 4: Sfr 110-175
Credit cards: AE, VS, DC, - all major
U.S.Representative: Utell International
Rep. Telephone No.: (800) 223-9868

I returned to the Wilden Mann with trepidation for I wondered if it could possibly compare in reality to the perfection of my memory. My worries were unwarranted. If anything the Wilden Mann was even more perfect than I had remembered. The hotel is unique, a genuine country inn - an oasis of charm and hospitality located in the heart of the medieval village of Lucerne. On this occasion I had the good fortune to meet Mr. Fritz Furler who is owner of the Wilden Mann. His time is very precious since he is constantly surveying the three hotels his family owns in Lucerne. Since the manager of the Wilden Mann was on a holiday, Mr. Furler did me the great honor of taking the time to give me some intriguing insights into the history of the hotel. We walked down to the dining room where there are three scenes created like miniature stage settings in glass frames. Each frame depicts a period in the history of the Wilden Mann as it has progressed from the year 1517 when it was built. Each scene shows dramatic changes - the most unusual perhaps is the first scene which shows a river running in front of the hotel complete with a drawbridge leading to the hotel entrance!

Mr Furler is a charming man. It is no wonder that his hotel is so delightful. He is totally aware of every detail of his hotel's operation. The Wilden Mann has been in the Furler family for many years. It is this continuity of ownership and love and devotion that makes hotels such as the Wilden Mann so extraordinary, more like a home than a hotel. The hotel has a "genuine" feel of quality to it with marvelous antiques everywhere, not only in the lobby and lounges but also scattered artistically throughout the halls. There are several restaurants within the hotel, each delightful in its own way. The "Liedertafel" is a French style restaurant with pink table clothes, candle light, and in cold weather a cozy fire. Upstairs there is an outdoor garden terrace where tables are set for dining on warm summer days. My favorite of the restaurants is the "Burgerstube". A cozy, charming, very Swiss country style dining room with an ambiance of informality and warmth. Here there are wooden chairs - many of them genuine antiques. The room's atmosphere is accented with wrought iron artifacts and colorful crests bordering the wall. Should you want to stop for a drink there is a tiny little bar on the second floor oozing with charm.

Since the Wilden Mann is such an old building the bedrooms vary considerably. If you are traveling with friends you might each have a room entirely different in size and style of decor. However this is one of the charms of the hotel. It is not a large commercial operation where everything has a stamp of "plastic" sameness. Instead, each bedroom varies as it would if you were a guest in a friend's home. The rooms I saw were delightful. It is no wonder since I understand that Mrs. Furler personally supervises the decorating down to the tiniest detail!

It is a joy to recommend a hotel with such sincerity. The Wilden Mann remains one of my favorite hotels and I think when you stay there it will become one of your favorites too.

WILDEN MANN HOTEL
Owner: Mr Fritz Furler
Manager: Mrs Susi Rick
Address: Bahnhofstrasse 30
           CH-6003 Lucerne
Phone: (041) 23 16 66   *Telex:* 78233
Dates open: All Year
No. rooms: 50   *With shower/bath:* 43
Rates: Double w/bath: Sfr 125-175
Credit cards: All Major cards
U.S.Representative: Romantik Hotels
Rep. Telephone No.: (800) 826-0015

If you are fortunate enough to sample the charms of this dear little inn, any appreciation and thanks should be directed to my good friend Carol. A true country inn wanderer, Carol is forever discovering hideaways all over the world! When asked about Switzerland, she raved to me about "her" little Albergo in Lugano. If anyone other that Carol had recommended the Albergo Ticino, I probably would have abandoned the effort to locate it. It proved a nuisance to circumvent the congested periphery of Lugano in an attempt to find the center of the old part of Lugano where the hotel is located, but with thoughts of Carol I persisted. How glad I was that I did, and again, how dependable and accurate Carol's description was!

The medieval section of Lugano is a marvelous maze of twisting alleys, stairways, streets (most closed to all but pedestrians), and a delightful confusion of little squares, restaurants, and boutiques. The Albergo Ticino is appropriately located right at the "heart" of the old city, on one of those little squares, surrounded by shops and local color. Although not far away, you must actually park your car and walk to the hotel, as it is in a section closed to traffic.

On the ground floor you will discover a tiny lobby and two individual, intimate dining rooms. The bedrooms, lounge areas and public rooms are found on the upper floors. Each level is bright with flowers, greenery and graced with some lovely paintings and handsome antiques. The Albergo Ticino is a wonderful old Tessin house, turned into a delightful hotel. It is owned and operated by the Buchmann family who effectively practice their motto " to serve is our duty - to serve well our pleasure." Carol was so right. What more could one desire in a small hotel?

HOTEL ALBERGO TICINO
Hotelier: Claire & Samuel Buchmann
Address: Piazza Cioccaro 1
         CH-6901 Lugano
Phone: (091) 22 77 72
Dates open: February to December
No. rooms: 23   *With shower/bath:* 23
Rates: Double room: Sfr 160-170
Credit cards: AE, VS
U.S.Representative: Romantik Hotels
Rep. Telephone No.: (800) 826-0015

 MORCOTE   *CARINA HOTEL*

The Carina Hotel is situated directly on the road facing Lake Lugano in the picturesque small village of Morcote, only about a half an hour drive south of Lugano. Across the street from the hotel is an outdoor cafe suspended on stilts out over the lake. Flowers and a brightly striped red and white awning add even further fun to this dining haven. An inside dining room has a wooden beamed ceiling, white walls accented by green plants, and a few well spaced antiques for accent and oriental rugs a very lovely room done with delightful taste. Upstairs there are several floors of bedrooms. The front rooms facing the lake might be noisy with the traffic, they would still be my first choice. I would rather trade quiet for the enchanting lake views. Quieter rooms are found in the back, many of which look out onto the small pool snuggled in the upper terrace above the hotel.

The Albergo Hotel Carina has another real advantage, the owner, Heidi Echsle. I did not have the opportunity to meet Mr Echsle, but his wife was at the reception desk when I arrived. Mrs Echsle speaks beautiful English and is so very friendly that I know a guest would feel immediately "at home". This is another hotel at which the owners are very involved with the management and the hotel shows their love and caring. As I walked through the hotel it looked like a meticulous housewife had just been through before me arranging lovely bouquets of flowers, adjusting each painting, fluffing each pillow. Each detail showed lovely taste and concern with the comfort of the guest in mind.

I want to go back to the Hotel Carina ... for an extended stay. Initially I would not leave the hotel premises, just sleep late and enjoy the view from the room before perhaps moving out to the terrace for lunch. Afterwards I might venture a little further, to visit the lovely park which is like a museum of gorgeous plants and little trails. The park, Parco Scherrer, is located just a five minute walk from the Carina. (You will need to double check the park's hours as they vary.) Perhaps then I'd be willing to explore the small villages clinging to the edge of the lake. The ferry boats ply the lake serving to join most of the little villages closer together. What fun to float from one charming town to another, getting off to sample the food from little water front cafes. What a perfect holiday it would be!

CARINA HOTEL
Hotelier: Heidi & Horst Echsle
Address: CH-6922 Morcote
Phone: (091) 69 11 31
Dates open: March to November
No. rooms: 19 *With shower/bath:* 14
Rates: Double room w/bath: Sfr 120-180
Credit cards: AE, VS, EC, DC

My anticipation was high as we drove up to to Le Vieux Manoir au Lac as I had already fallen in love with the image projected by the brochure. I was not disappointed. The hotel is a wonderful combination of weathered wood, stucco, little gables, high pitched roofs, overhanging eaves and whimsical chimneys, harmonizing to produce a cozy welcome. As I was waiting to check in, I heard a couple at the front desk raving to the receptionist that they had enjoyed the best meal of their entire Swiss sojourn while staying at Le Vieux Manoir au Lac. This was a wonderful introduction and promise of what was to be a memorable stay!

Le Vieux Manoir has a serene setting. A lush green lawn dotted with shade trees stretches down from the hotel to the lake and the swans and ducks. It was so enjoyable seeing a mother swan swimming gently in the water followed by her three fluffy little babies. She portrayed an image of tranquillity until some careless ducks had the impertinence to maneuver too close to her brood and she ferociously screeched at them before returning to her peaceful drifting.

A warm, sunny day completed what seemed a perfect welcome. Our room, which looked out over the expanse of lawn and the peaceful lake, was small but nicely decorated with a provincial print that covered the walls, ceiling and extended into the dressing area and bathroom. I wanted to inspect more of the rooms, but since they were all occupied I had to be satisfied with quick glimpses over the shoulders of a few maids as they readied them for the next guests. The manager's wife, Mrs Thomas, was very helpful and shared with me a few of her favorites. I was told that room number 6 has a large canopy bed and lovely balcony, and room number 24 enjoys a lake view and its own little alcove. However, Mrs. Thomas mentioned the difficulty in selecting a "favorite" , as improvements and changes are continuously being made. A new turret wing is being built and will soon provide some of the inn's loveliest rooms. Therefore, she suggested that one write and simply state a preference of style when making reservations, and let them assist you in the choice depending, of course, on availability.

That night our dinner was truly gourmet. There were several choices for complete dinners, most of which were quite expensive. However, since we were not extremely hungry we ate a la carte and had a delicious meal of fresh fish and a green salad. It was skillfully served, and the atmosphere of the dining room was romantic with lovely table settings and fresh flowers. The end to a perfect day.

LE VIEUX MANOIR AU LAC
Hotelier: Mr Erich Thomas
Address: CH-3280 Murten-Meyriez
Phone: (037) 71 12 83   *Telex:* 942 026
Dates open: February-December
No. rooms: 23
Rates: Double room: Sfr 140-180
        Suites: Sfr 210-250
Credit cards: VS, DC
U.S.Representative: David B. Mitchell
Rep. Telephone No.: (415) 546-1311/SFO
            (212) 696-1323/NYC

 MUSTAIR   *HOTEL CHASA CHALAVAINA*

I thought one lovely hotel in the the beautiful Mustair Valley would be sufficient for this guide, and since I had just fallen in love with the CHASA CAPOL, in the village of Santa Maria I was not going to search further. However the weather was so gorgeous that I decided to travel the extra few miles to Mustair, and found another divine inn, so charming that it begged to be included in this book. Although only a few miles from CHASA CAPOL, CHASA CHALAVAINA is quite different with a charm all of its own. Fresh white walls and an open, uncluttered decor gave the hotel a crisp airy atmosphere. The dining room is decorated with the wonderful wooden country style furniture and also includes an old ceramic stove so often seen in old inns. I struggled to explain to the owner, Mr. Jon Fasser, who unfortunately for me did not speak English, that I would like permission to take photos and to see some bedrooms. We were not communicating too well when I was approached by a charming Swiss lady, obviously a guest at the hotel, who had been listening to the conversation and eagerly offered to assist. She delayed her departure of a day's excursion to take me under her wing and personally show me the entire hotel. First we saw her room, delightful with country style decor and a beautiful balcony overlooking the valley. My new found friend and I then peeked into every nook and cranny (luckily most of the guests were already out for the day) , including the kitchen, dining rooms and bar. After the "tour" my friend rejoined her husband whom she had deposited at the hotel's arched entrance, said goodbye and was on her way. I still wonder what Mr. Fasser must have thought about this strange couple wandering around his hotel!. Although it was a bit embarrassing at the time, I was glad to have found another excellent inn.

HOTEL CHASA CHALAVAINA
Hotelier: Jon Fasser
Address: CH-7537 Mustair
Phone: (082) 8 54 68
Dates open: All Year
No. rooms: 20
Rates: Double room: Sfr 53-80

The Hotel Du Clos Sadex is located about fifteen miles from Geneva on the north shore of Lake Geneva. Surrounded by its own quiet expanse of gardens, the hotel's address is written as Nyon, but it is actually on the main, lakeside road, just a short distance east of the town. Once an elegant patrician estate, it serves now as an elegant hotel. The entrance would profit from a little fresh paint, and the bedrooms, although, bright and spacious could also use a little sprucing up. However there is a casual, loveable charm to this small hotel. The staff is extremely hospitable and cordial, and the downstairs public rooms are very cozy and charming. Oriental rugs enrich wooden, parquet floors and antiques are handsomely displayed throughout. The bedrooms are divided between the main house and an adjacent annex. Amidst trees, flowers and surrounded by green lawns, you will love the setting of the Hotel Clos de Sadex and enjoy the feeling of being a guest in a private home.

HOTEL DU CLOS DE SADEX
Hotelier: L. de Tscharner
Address: CH-1260 Nyon
Phone: (022) 61 28 31
Dates open: March - January
No. rooms: 15
Rates: Double room: Sfr 96-190

The Rote Rose is my idea of *THE PERFECT INN*. The manager, Christa Schafer is one of the most charming, delightful women I have had the pleasure to meet in my travels. It has an idyllic setting on the knoll of a hill with a splendid view. It has a unique position in the middle of a medieval village with the wonderful ambiance of a beautifully restored historic building. It has intrigue in that the owners of the Rote Rose were horribly persecuted for crusading to preserve the unique town of Regensberg. It has exquisitely furnished antique decor with one of the Switzerland's finest gourmet restaurants next door. And if this were not enough, it is owned by Lotte Gunthart, a world famous rose artist whose contribution to the world of roses has been so significant that there is even a rose named after her!

I had read about the Rote Rose and certainly knew it was an inn I wanted to visit. My first impression of this truly unique hotel was when I called to make my reservation. Christa Schafer, who manages the Rote Rose, answered the telephone and immediately knew who I was from earlier correspondence, and was so delightfully gracious that I felt very special. Christa Schafer, young and pretty and vivacious, is Lotte Gunthart's daughter. After sharing only a short while with her on two occasions, I feel we are friends.

The wonderful medieval walled town of Regensberg is conveniently located only twenty-five minutes from Zurich. it is a perfect village originating from the year 1245 when it was founded by the Baron Lutold V. I don't know who Lutold was, but he certainly knew a beautiful location when he found it! The town is so perfectly situated on the hill top that there is a 360 degree view.

The Rote Rose was reconstructed from one of the old houses. Downstairs there is an art gallery of Lotte Gunthart's paintings and a gift shop. I had read articles about Lotte Gunthart's fame as a rose artist, but I did not realize how clever she is in so many fields. She has illustrated children's books with wonderful whimsical drawings, illustrated gourmet cookbooks, published books on roses, does portrait painting, figure drawing - the list goes on and on of this talented woman's accomplishments. I had the pleasure to meet Lotte Gunthart and share a cup of tea on the balcony of the inn. I could immediately see where her daughter derived her charm. Her mother too is a beautiful person with the special quality of sincere warmth and hospitality.

This little inn only has two suites. Each suite has one bedroom, a small sitting room, and a kitchenette where snacks can be served and the ingredients are left for morning breakfast. One of the suites has a romantic four poster double bed, the other suite suite has twin beds, both with lovely panoramic views of the countryside below. If any fault could be found for the Rote Rose, it would be that a tall person must be careful not to bump his head on the low ceilings. (However, I might add that this inn is worth "bending a little!")

In addition to the two suites there is an antique filled reception area up a flight of stairs from the shop. This is just beautiful with antiques of the highest quality artfully displayed. In the main salon there is a porch-like balcony with little tables set for snacks and with a fairytale view.

The Rote Rose has no restaurant within the building. But do not despair! Right next door the Guntharts also own and manage the Gasthaus Krone, one of the most beautiful restaurants I have ever seen with antiques galore, dramatic displays of fresh flowers, gourmet cooking, and impeccable service. It is really too much to describe. You will just have to go yourself.

I mentioned there was also intrigue in this history of the Rote Rose. The story of what anguish the Gunthart family went through to preserve this unique, perfect village is amazing. The story emphasizes that this family is not only warm and gracious, they are also strong and willing to suffer for what they know is right. The Gunthart family moved to Regensberg about thirty-four years ago loving the unique quality of this "Storybook Perfect" hamlet. When the town council approved the construction of a highrise concrete and glass housing development on the slopes of the hillside beneath the old town walls, the Guntharts were astounded. One now wonders how anyone would have to go to battle to preserve this beautiful town against the invasion of highrise monstrosities - the consequence seems so obvious - but battle was unfortunately necessary. The Guntharts knew that the highrise would forever destroy this town. The battle was not short. Each time one campaign was concluded a battle erupted in another sector. The town fathers wanted to build a housing development, then a prison below the town, then a large parking garage. The battles went on and on. Painfully ugly battles with the local townspeople who wanted "progress" persisting against the Guntharts who knew that the short lived commercial gains of this particular kind of progress would forever destroy this irreplaceable "Living Museum". Lotte Gunthart told me that her family could not walk down the street without encountering hostility. Hate letters were received regularly. One day a dead rose was put on the doorstep with its obvious implication. Perhaps the seriousness of the situation was demonstrated when Christa Schafer was expecting her second child and some fanatic fired a gun into her bedroom luckily missing her. Most would have given up, but not the Guntharts. The battle went on for years. They had to live amidst hatred and ridicule, but finally they won and for the last ten years there has been peace. Not only peace, but actual compliance of the town which now not only no longer fights the Guntharts, but have "jumped on the bandwagon". Everywhere little houses in the village are being reconstructed, beautiful flower gardens are planted, the whole quality of the town improving.

Finally the town has realized that the Guntharts were right in their perseverance. Not only were they correct esthetically and morally to protect this town from destruction, but economically they were right. As tourists now flock to visit this enchanting town, the money comes in too. I should guess that the town is benefiting more from the impact of tourism than it ever would have from the highrises proposed. My respect and love goes out to the very talented and special Gunthart Family.

ROTE ROSE
Owner: Lotte & Willi Gunthart
Manager: Christa Schafer
Address: CH-8158 Regensberg
Phone: (01) 853 1013 in AM (01) 853 0080
No. rooms: 2 *With shower/bath:* 2
Rates: USD $ 70

GASTHOF BAREN is a must if you are driving through the glorious Kandertal Valley at lunch or dinnertime. It is a special inn, with spectacular food served in an ideal setting. Everything is perfect and done with exquisite taste. The entrance is via a paneled wooden hallway. There are several dining rooms each a picture of the "typical Swiss inn". The walls are wood paneled, each dining area done in Swiss country wooden style, antique tiled stoves in the corners, dinner plates on display on the walls, crisp white curtains complemented by dark green draperies covering the casement windows giving a total feel of country elegance. My thoughts that I had "discovered" a very special hotel were quickly erased when at dinner the dining room was packed with obviously very discriminating diners, some of whom had traveled from nearby cities for an excellent meal. Jacob Murner, whose family owns the inn, is not only the magnificent chef but also a fantastic host. Throughout the evening he appeared periodically to ensure the guests were well attended and happy. He told us of the stringent training required by chefs in Switzerland to produce gourmet food with such a professional touch. The standard minimum training is to apprentice for 3 years with an accredited chef, then various tests and supplemental courses have to be taken. No wonder the quality of dining through Switzerland is so excellent!

The very simple hotel rooms are located across the street from the restaurant. Although none of the bedrooms have private baths, they do have so much potential that they would make a decorator crave the opportunity to use new wallpaper, carpets, and fresh paint etc., something Mr. Murner has plans for in the future. The furnishings are highlighted by some special antique pieces, especially in rooms 1, 8 and 9.

At this time though I recommend the inn principally as a wonderful dining stop. In our travels throughout Switzerland we rarely found such a warm and accommodating hosts as Mr. and Mrs. Murner. Please introduce yourselves to them. They speak beautiful English and will make your visit an enjoyable one. You will not only have a marvelous meal but will have experienced true Swiss hospitality.

GASTHOF BAREN
Hotelier: Jacob Murner
Address: CH-3713 Reichenbach
Phone: (033) 76 12 51
Dates open: June 1st to October 31st
No. rooms: 13   *With shower/bath:* 13
Rates: Double room: Sfr 30

 SAAS-FEE   *WALDHOTEL FLETSCHHORN*

Getting to the Waldhotel Fletschhorn was an adventure! I had always wondered if the little valleys parallel to the Zermatt valley held equally wonderful little hamlets. Therefore, it was with a real sense of anticipation that I left the Rhone Valley highway at Visp and took the the road south toward Zermatt. This time when the road split, I took the left branch toward Saas-Fee instead of going right toward Zermatt.

The road which leads to Saas-Fee is glorious with green fields, dramatic mountain gorges, rushing rivers, and old weathered wood chalets. I kept thinking we had arrived at our destination for every little village indicated our proximity - Saas-Balen, Saas-Grund, and Saas-Almagell. Just when I thought we were at the end of the valley the road veered to the right and began to climb up the mountain. It seemed like we were in some "hidden" Shangri-la, so what a shock it was to see road markers to PARKING LOT NUMBER ONE and PARKING LOT NUMBER TWO! Obviously we were not the first to venture into this lovely valley. A little disappointed, we parked the car and then wondered how we would ever find the Waldhotel Fletschhorn. But the Swiss triumphed again in making life very easy for the traveler. Next to the parking terminal number one and across from the bus station is the tourist office. On the outside of the tourist office is a large map of Saas-Fee indicating location of all of the hotels by little lights. When a button is pushed the corresponding red button lights up on the map to indicate your hotel. When you punch another button by your hotel's name you are automatically connected by telephone to the hotel of your choice. How simple! Since it looked like a long walk to the the Waldhotel Fletschhorn we were afraid of becoming lost, so we rang the hotel eagerly accepting the owner's offer to come and retrieve us. He instructed us to wait at the tourist office and sure enough in about ten minutes Mr Dutsch arrived with his daughter Sandra in an electric cart.

After seeing the huge concrete parking areas, I was concerned that the town of Saas-Fee would be extremely disappointing, but as we rolled through the little town it was very picturesque and beautifully positioned on a little plateau high up the mountain.

Hansjorg Dutsch, who speaks beautiful English, asked if we minded if he stopped to pick up some fresh vegetables as we drove through town. We were delighted since it gave us a few minutes to browse in the little shops which were mostly filled with items for hiking or skiing. After a quick stop at the market, we were on our way again. As we left the village we drove through an open field with many new hotels and condominium projects following the Swiss chalet motif of architecture. After a clearing in the meadow we drove through a dense forest for about five minutes and suddenly there appeared before us in a field all by itself the Waldhotel Fletschhorn beautifully situated on a plateau with a gorgeous view out over the valley.

The hotel was full of guests. In addition to not being the first person to "discover" Saas-Fee, I was obviously not the first person to discover the Waldhotel Fletschhorn! All the rooms were occupied so Sandra gave us her room for the night and she moved in with her sister Caroline. I did however get a chance to see some of the other rooms which vary in style and decor. Room number 6 was very pleasant with an enormous bathroom and a balcony with a lovely view. My favorite though was room number 15 all alone on a lower level below the parking lot. This room had a fairytale view of the valley plus a cozy red checked gingham decor.

One of the hotel's best features has been saved for last. Here in the middle of "nowhere" is a woman gourmet cook proclaimed to be the best in Switzerland. She is Irma Dutsch, the owner's wife. Irma is not only an incredible cook, but she also sparkles with personality and makes her guests feel like personal friends whom she is pleased to welcome into her home. When I asked her more details on her reputation as a gourmet chef, she showed me photographs of some of her culinary creations being used in television programs, and clippings from various magazines around the world. Also, "Gourmet Magazine" is contemplating featuring the charm of this isolated inn and the the delicacies prepared by Irma Dutsch. At dinner Irma promised to prepare a selection of her delicacies for us. I could not believe my eyes at' what appeared! Seven courses arrived - each more beautifully displayed than the previous one. Exotic, delicious entrees such as quail's egg souffle with lobster sauce! During one course I was admiring the beautiful flower design on my plate, only to realize on closer inspection that actually I was eating off two plates. The lower plate was white china with an artistic arrangement of fresh wild flowers. A clear crystal plate was pressed on top through which the flowers below showed through in an exquisite design. I should mention that that this dinner was "special" for us. However, as I looked about me the "standard" dinners looked absolutely delicious and beautifully prepared.

I really cannot close my description of the Waldhotel Fletschhorn without mentioning the dessert served at dinner. On a large plate was arranged a selection of mousses and parfaits and sorbets. These were arranged like a flower with seven petals, each a different color - one petal a chocolate mousse, one petal a plum parfait, one petal a lime sorbet, etc. etc. My final thought as we reluctantly left the Waldhotel Fletschhorn was that thank goodness there were so many beautiful walking trails leading off from the hotel - with Irma Dutsch's gourmet cooking walking would be a prerequisite for survival!

WALDHOTEL FLETSCHHORN
Hotelier: Hansjorg Dutsch
Address: CH-3906 Saas-Fee
Phone: (028) 57 21 31
No. rooms: 10   *With shower/bath:* 10
Rates: Double room: Sfr 138-182,
          On a demi-pension basis

 29 **SACHSELN**   *HOTEL KREUZ*

I almost lost the chance to include a truly wonderful hotel. Toward the end of a long day of hotel inspections, I had been going into one inn after another only to find darling, flower bedecked exteriors hiding dismal interiors. As we drove through the town of Sachseln it did not look too exciting and I saw nothing resembling an inn on the main road. My conscience overcame my weariness and we circled back through the town to look again for the Hotel Kreuz which I had on my list of "maybes". The Kreuz Hotel, a few blocks off the main highway, did not look too promising from the outside. It is rather a stately old manor home behind which is a rather uninteresting motel section. However, what a surprise inside! Although a rather large hotel it is delightfully decorated with great charm. The hotel has been in the same family since 1489! Family antiques are everywhere - old chests, wonderful clocks, cradles, armories, paintings, antique tables, beautiful old chairs, and other heirlooms highlight the tasteful decor in all the public rooms.

The manager, Mr. Lotzing, was most hospitable. I was almost afraid to ask to see some of the bedrooms for fear that they would be a great disappointment. The first few rooms Mr. Lotzing showed me were pleasant but not outstanding. I asked if perhaps some of the rooms had a little more "character". I was then shown toa old wooden Swiss chalet located adjacent to the main hotel. I had thought that this was not actually a part of the hotel but a completely separate home. However it belongs to the same family, and the present patriarch of the family, in his eighties, has an apartment on the lower floor where he comes to stay when he is not at his home in Geneva. Rooms number 1 and 2 in this little cottage are lovingly restored and decorated in simple country style, very appropriate for a house dating back 400 years! This little wooden chalet is called the "colored house" because it used to be painted red which signified that this was the home of the magistrate - the most important man in town.
Mr. Lotzing then gave me another surprise. In the rear of the main residence is an old mill which has also been converted into hotel rooms. Here is one of the most beautifully decorated rooms I had seen in Switzerland - suite # 73. If you want to splurge ask for this suite as it is really special.

The town of Sachseln is situated on the pretty little Lake Sarnen where the hotel has its own garden area right on the shore, only a five minute walk from the hotel. There are many country walking trails branching out from Sachseln which would be most enjoyable on a sunny day.

HOTEL KREUZ
Hotelier: Mr. E.H. Lotzing
Address: CH-6072 Sachseln
Phone: (041) 661 466   *Telex:* 72643
Dates open: All Year
No. rooms: 50   *With shower/bath:* 40
Rates: Double room: Sfr 60-110
Credit cards: AE, VS, DC, EC

 55 **SANTA MARIA**   *HOTEL CHASA CAPOL*

The Chasa Capol is a unique hotel located on the main street of the small town of Santa Maria in the beautiful Mustair Valley. The colorful background of the inn given to me by the owner stated :

"The foundation of Chasa Capol dates back to the 8th Century. Over the centuries, it was the property of the noble family *DE CAPOL* as well as the governors residence of the valley. The Capol's genealogical tree has been traced back to the Venetian Marco Polo - One ancestor was a disciple of the Holy Sebastianus. In 1506 the boundary settlement of the "Schwabenkreig" War between Emperor Maximilianus and Colonel Capol of the Grisons took place in this house. Today the romantic Hotel Chasa Capol remains as a cultural and artistic meeting place of discriminating guests."

The hotel's history piqued my imagination, and it alone would have merited a visit to this beautiful remote valley. I loved the Chasa Capol from the moment I walked into the small lobby and was warmly welcomed. The owners, Mr and Mrs. Ernst Schweizer, speak no English, but their smile of welcome is an international language. They do have a darling young lady who has been with them for many years who does speak English which will make your stay easier if you need sightseeing suggestions, etc.

The rooms have names which represent famous guests. Our room, "Guerg Jenatsch", overlooked the back garden. There were twin beds joined by a wooden headboard painted green with reading lamps on either side. On the beds were the ever present fluffy down comforters covered with a delightful red and green provincial print fabric plus a small writing table with chair and lamp. Rag rugs on the floor and cheerful green print draperies on the window completed the scene. The decor was not deluxe, but simple, clean and inviting.

The dining room was charming with light antique wood furniture, flowers everywhere and wonderful food. Mrs. Schweizer is an accomplished chef who adds her talents in personally supervising the kitchen. To complement the meal the Chasa Capol has its own vineyards and serve an excellent Gewurtztraminer house wine. They even have their own casks of wine stored in the cellar!

The hotel has a small pool in the rear garden which would be a pleasant addition on a warm summer day if traveling with children.

Dating back to the 8th century qualifies this inn as one of the oldest buildings in this book. The Schweizers are lovingly restoring this wonderful historical building. The hotel almost has a museum quality with a small chapel in the basement with precious icons, a cute little theatre in the attic where special concerts are still given, plus artifacts throughout such as antique costumes and old sleds. Staying at the Chasa Capol is truly like stepping back 1000 years to enjoy the ambiance of yesterday with the amenities of today.

HOTEL CHASA CAPOL
Hotelier: Mr & Mrs Ernest Schweizer
Address: CH-7536 Santa Maria
Phone: (082) 8 57 28
Dates open: All Year
No. rooms: 20   *With shower/bath:* 20
Rates: Double room: Sfr 90-150

 SATIGNY *AUBERGE DE CHATEAUVIEUX*

The Auberge de Chateauvieux is located just a twenty minute drive from the Geneva airport and would be a convenient hotel choice for a first night in Switzerland. It is difficult to comprehend that you are only a few miles west of a large city as you approach this thirteenth century stone manor. On the knoll of a hill laced with fields of vineyards, it seems miles from a cosmopolitan center.

In the courtyard is an old wine press and in the summer an abundance of bright flowers. Inside the Auberge de Chateauvieux there is a lovely dining room with a tasteful array of antiques intermingled with the new to give a feeling of coziness and warmth. Upstairs there are only a few bedrooms, all tastefully decorated, some with lovely views out over the vineyards.

For those who prefer country living to the big cities the Auberge de Chateauvieux would be a very good alternative to staying in Geneva. You could have best of two worlds by staying in the country with only a short drive into Geneva for sightseeing.

AUBERGE DE CHATEAUVIEUX
Hotelier: Mr Alfred Bossotto
Address: Penny-Dessus
            CH-1242 Satigny
Phone: (022) 53 14 45
Dates open: Jan 10-Aug10, Aug 20-Dec20
No. rooms: 12   *With shower/bath:* 12
Rates: Double room: Sfr 100-120
Credit cards: AE, VS, DC, EC
U.S.Representative: Romantik Hotels
Rep. Telephone No.: (800) 826-0015

SCHAFFHAUSEN   *RHEINHOTEL FISCHERZUNFT*

Although I had read about the Rheinhotel Fischerzunft in several books, I still feel it is my "discovery"! None of the books raved about the hotel. In fact, several seemed to imply that the hotel left much to be desired. Because the location (directly on the Rhine adjacent to the ferry landing in the medieval walled city of Schaffhausen) sounded so spectacular, I decided the hotel Fischerzunft deserved a quick look.

As soon as I saw the hotel I was impressed. The hotel is freshly painted and looks sparkling clean and immaculate from the outside. The day I was there, the sun was glorious and shone invitingly on a small outdoor patio to the side of the hotel. Inside the Rheinhotel Fischerzunft radiates warmth and atmosphere. A gorgeous dining room to the left of the entry was bustling with activity. What appeared to be a private men's luncheon occupied the lounge room. Decorated in rich, muted colors, the lounge is handsome and the gentlemen were immersed in their own conversation and settled in as if in a private residence. From the way all the guests appeared so comfortable and "at home", I knew the hotel had to be very special.

Mrs Jaeger, the owner's wife welcomed me. Those lucky enough to arrive before me had already reserved every room, therefore I had to be content just looking about. The hotel is done with impeccable taste and shows loving care in every detail. Until a century ago, the building used to house a fisherman's guild. At that time it was converted to a restaurant and then about fifty years ago it was expanded into a hotel. However, it was only two years ago that the Jaegers finished the renovation. Their exquisite taste is responsible for making the hotel so remarkably attractive. I am sure they must be proud of their accomplishment. The Rheinhotel Fischerzunft is truly a gem!

RHEINHOTEL FISCHERZUNFT
Hotelier: Andre & Doreen Jaeger-Soong
Address: Rheinquai 8
          CH-8200 Schaffhausen
Phone: (053) 5 32 81
Dates open: Feb 22nd to Jan 31st
No. rooms: 7   *With shower/bath:* 7
Rates: Double room: Sfr 130-165
Credit cards: AE, DC, VS, MC
U.S.Representative: David B. Mitchell
Rep. Telephone No.: (415) 546-1311/SFO
          (212) 696-1323/NYC

Caught between a busy winter season and the beginning of the beautiful summer season, the Alpenrose was closed briefly on my first visit to the Gstaad area. I was glad that there were no meandering law officers in the area as I peeked in windows and climbed up on the decks trying to evaluate the facilities and give you a "picture" of a hotel whose reputation is one of a delightful, small, family establishment. I was unable to see any of the bedrooms since they appeared to be on the upper floors and I decided it wise not to attempt the climb necessary to get a first hand view. Studying the brochure, the bedrooms seem to be small but cozy with wood paneled walls, provincial patterned draperies, and fluffy down comforters encased in fabric of matching prints. I was able to see the lower rooms decorated with a happy country charm. This small inn is located directly on the main highway. However, to the rear is a lovely terrace opening out to the mountain vistas.

I think you can get a "feeling" of the very personal caring and atmosphere of the Alpenrose from the following description from the owner.

"The Alpenrose has been my home for over thirty years. Monique and I and our children live in the house. Therefore we have extra incentive to make it attractive and pleasant. Monique's taste in Alpine peasant art has been given further expression in her small boutique.

We went to a lot of trouble to arrange our restaurant so that I could personally prepare some of our specialities, and simultaneously enjoy the company of our guests ... because, frankly, cooking good food is as much my hobby as my profession. We've tried to make the Alpenrose combine comfort, food and drink we're proud to serve, and a nice clientele. Our hotel accommodations are not extensive, but are quiet and comfortable. We hope to welcome you personally soon. Family F. von Siebenthal-Gobeli."

What more can I add to these simple words of welcome.

HOTEL ALPENROSE
Hotelier: Monika Von Siebenthal-Gobeli
Address: CH-3778 Schonried-Gstaad
Phone: (030) 4 12 38
Dates open: June-Nov and Dec-April
No. rooms: 4   *With shower/bath:* 4
Rates: Double room: Sfr 100-200
Credit cards: VS, DC, EC

 37 SCHONRIED-GSTAAD *HOTEL ERMITAGE GOLF SOLBAD*

The Hotel Ermitage Golf Solbad can legitimately be considered one of the "real" Swiss inns. The exterior is in keeping with the traditional chalet style and the core of the complex is very wonderful, very old and very Swiss. Additional wings extend to either side, but architecturally the hotel manages to preserve the atmosphere of the original building. What a delight to find that the great standard of style has been continued inside. An inviting lounge area is warmed by a fireplace and the dining room is beautifully paneled and enhanced by crisp white curtains, white table linens and cheerful flower arrangements.

The bedrooms are modernly furnished, and if you are able to reserve a room with a view, you will be afforded a splendid unobstructed panoramas of the gorgeous Swiss Alps rising across the meadow! The Ermitage Golf Solbad has so many modern amenities (a sauna, fitness/massage center, squash, tennis courts, golf course) that in a way I hesitated to recommend it for fear that it far exceeded the definition of "country inn", but after a long day of sightseeing, I found the facilities a welcome relief! It is also such a pleasure to find a hotel so conscientiously modernized in such exquisite taste!

HOTEL ERMITAGE GOLF SOLBAD
Owner: H. Lutz
Manager: L. Schmid
Address: CH-3778 Schonried-Gstaad
Phone: (030) 4 27 27   *Telex:* 922 213
Dates open: May-Nov and Dec-April
No. rooms: 45   *With shower/bath:* 45
Rates: Double room: Sfr 200-310 on a
        demi-pension basis
Credit cards: AE, VS, DC

 SILS-BASELGIA *HOTEL MARGNA*

In my wanderings it was rare to come across a "gem" of a hotel which was not already referenced by another source. Rather, it seemed I spent most of my travels investigating and then having to delete described "gems". So I was pleased to simply happen upon the Hotel Margna as we drove by.

I really did not expect too much as I had become rather cynical about what I would find inside some of my "discoveries". Therefore, it was an absolute delight when I entered the hotel and found the lobby very tasteful in its decor with extremely professional and friendly personnel at the reception desk.

As I wandered from room to room my appreciation of the Hotel Margna grew. Each room is delightful with warm, cream colored walls, antique accents such as an old sleigh laden with flowers, oriental rugs, a cozy lounge with fireplace and a beautiful dining room with a beamed ceiling. The few guest rooms I saw were charming with the same ambiance found throughout the hotel. Number 49 has an exceptional view across the meadows and lake.

The Hotel Margna is truly a country hotel with a gracious touch of sophistication. It also had the advantage of being able to offer the niceties of a larger hotel. There are several lounges , a grill restaurant with an open fireplace, plus a second dining room - the Stuva. The hotel has game rooms, a television lounge, and even a sauna.

Originally a large private residence, the Hotel Margna was built in 1817 by Johann Josty, who returned here, homesick for the Engadine. Beautifully situated between two lakes, Johann took advantage of what must have been the most spectacular lot available. In the summertime there are countless paths along the lakefront or leading up to imposing mountain peaks. In the winter it is a cross country skier's paradise and the world famous resort of St Moritz is just a few miles away. Often as I have written about hotels I have included them knowing that the fussy traveler might not like the rustic nature of the hotel. Not so with the Hotel Margna. Anyone would like it. It is delightful.

HOTEL MARGNA
Hotelier: Sepp & Dorly Muessgens
Address: CH-7515 Sils-Baselgia
Phone: (082) 4 53 06   *Telex:* 74 496
Dates open: Jun-Oct and Dec-Apr
No. rooms: 72   *With shower/bath:* 72
Rates: Double room: Sfr 75-120

 SILVAPLANA   *LA STAILA*

The ski resort of St Moritz attracts the wealthy, international jet set and is always alive with activity. The town, in my estimation, is too much of a hodge podge of styles and tastes jumbled together with new condominiums and nondescript hotels. St. Moritz is nestled amongst towering, snow capped mountain peaks and tucked in a little valley that is graced by a glistening lake. In the winter, iced with snow, the lake is a fairytale setting for sleigh races and skating. I have unsuccessfully searched in the past for a wonderful little inn to recommend in St Moritz. This time I extended by search and was extremely pleased to find a marvelous little inn only a few miles away. The ardent skier might still want to be right at the tram of St Moritz, but for those who prefer some charm in their accommodations, the answer might well be to overnight at Silvaplana which is only about four miles away.

Mr and Mrs Gut took over the La Staila Hotel a few years ago and have tastefully turned La Staila into a delightful inn. The reception area is small and friendly with antiques used to accent the decor. The dining room is especially charming with dark wooden chairs, white table cloths, and fresh flowers.

The bedrooms are all nice but they vary in style. My preference are the rooms, such as number 9 or 10, located in the original part of the hotel that are richly paneled in wood.

Even though it was my first introduction to the Hotel La Staila, I cannot claim it as my discovery. Mrs Gut informed me that the day before she had been visited by one of Stephen Birnbaum's staff writers. I admire the travel writer Mr Birnbaum very much and so felt my itinerary was following "good company".

LA STAILA
Hotelier: Familie Gut
Address: CH-7513 Silvaplana
Phone: (082) 48 147   *Telex:* 74855
No. rooms: 15   *With shower/bath:* 12
Rates: double room: Sfr 96-112

I cannot remember when I first learned of Soglio, but I have a mental picture of a small town clinging to a narrow ledge, perched high above a beautiful mountain valley. The postcard image is complete with church spire and cattle grazing on the surrounding hillsides. The memory of this village was tucked away with the conviction that one day I would visit Soglio and evaluate for myself the seeming perfection of this Swiss village.

A photographer's dream, Soglio, hanging to a small ledge above the Bregaglia Valley, is in reality as romantically beautiful as it is photogenic. I arrived in this small hamlet without a reservation. I had to cross three mountain passes first, and so was not at all certain how to estimate the amount of time the drive would demand. It was late afternoon when I reached the town and went directly to the Hotel Palazzo Salis. All the rooms in the main building were reserved but Mrs Cadisch, the owner, said that a room was available in one of the annexes. Evidently the hotel uses many rooms scattered about the village to service an overflow. I noticed many guests retiring to their rooms and disappearing from the lobby into other houses.

With the exception of the room I occupied, I was unable to see any others. It would be my guess that all the rooms would be as charming in their simplicity as ours - immaculately clean with down comforters on the beds. The hotel dates back several centuries and maintains a character of yester-year. A number of hunting trophies proudly decorate the reception area, and a collection of antique spears are artistically arranged on the third floor walls. The dining room is a cheerful cluster of small tables and its walls are hung with a series of mountain water colors. Behind the hotel is a delightful garden restaurant for warm weather dining.

I recommend the Hotel Palazzo Salis, but I apologize for the fact that I have not personally seen enough rooms to accurately describe the accommodations. However my room in the annex was delightful and the hotel fits perfectly into this fairytale village. Settle here and days can be spent following an endless number of paths that explore this gloriously beautiful region. I fell in love with Soglio and consider it one of Switzerland's most picturesque villages and well worth any detour.

HOTEL PALAZZO SALIS
Hotelier: Familie Cadisch
Address: CH-7649 Soglio
Phone: (082) 4 12 08
Dates open: April-October
No. rooms: 15
Rates: Double room: Sfr 78-84

 **SOLOTHURN**   *HOTEL KRONE*

The Hotel Krone is located in the fascinating, walled, medieval town of Solothurn. The building is everything a Swiss inn should be. A cozy exterior with the palest, soft, pink facade with contrasting muted green shutters fronted by window boxes overflowing with geraniums set the quiet mood of the inn. The location too is perfect - facing onto the colorful main square, just opposite Saint Urs Cathedral.

Inside, the reception area was more formal than the exterior would indicate, but the warmth of our greeting was not formal. The dining room has a cozy country inn atmosphere and fresh flowers are plentiful in the table settings. Upstairs, a large room is often used for private parties, and there is also a relaxing bar, perfect for a welcome drink. Outside, tables are set in good weather for light meals. The bedrooms are all very similar in decor with copies of Louis XV furniture that blend nicely with genuine antiques. The prices of the rooms fall basically in two categories. The more expensive rooms are enormous, about seventeen feet square and the bathrooms have tubs that one could practically swim in. The smaller rooms logically have a smaller price, but are similar in the rather formal decor. For the difference in price, the larger rooms are without a doubt a better value. For someone traveling alone, there are a few very reasonable single rooms.

Built in the thirteenth century the Krone Hotel was once the residence of the Ambassador of France and remains today as a very special hotel in a very special city.

HOTEL KRONE
Hotelier: Joseph Kung-Roschi
Address: Hauptgasse 64
              CH-4500 Solothurn
Phone: (065) 22 44 12
Dates open: All Year
No. rooms: 44   *With shower/bath:* 44
Rates: Double room: Sfr 100-160
Credit cards: AE, DC, VS, EC

It was September when I visited the Hotel Rosalp. Being a skier, I was eager to visit the famous jet set resort of Verbier. I could already get a feeling of what winter must be like for there was an early snowfall, the air was crisp and the mountain tops were glistening in pristine beauty.

The town of Verbier is located on a high meadow overlooking the Bagnes Valley. The Mont Blanc Massifs crown the view. It is known to long distance cross country skiers as the starting point of the "High Road Run", of which Saas-Fee or Zermatt is the terminus. I had always heard that Verbier was a modern town built expressly to satisfy the whims of the ardent skier. Therefore, I was pleased and surprised to notice as the car twisted up the road from the valley the many traditional wooden farm houses that remain and add character to the otherwise modern ski facilities.

As the road winds through the village of Verbier, you will see the Hotel Rosalp on your left, a typical chalet style hotel with the ever welcome small outdoor cafe in front. The entrance is small and opens up to a marvelous dining room with beautiful wood paneling and tables emphasizing the charming decor with crisp linens and fresh flowers. The overall effect is one of style and chic. It is easy to visualize sun tanned skiers enjoying an elegant dinner with a local wine after a day on the slopes.

All the bedrooms have private baths and are modern in their decor. However, it is the dining that really makes this hotel so very special. The owner, Roland Pierroz, has the reputation of serving some of the very finest food in Switzerland. Although I was not fortunate enough to personally sample the menu, other very fine Swiss hoteliers paid Mr Pierroz the highest compliment - they raved that " Mr Pierroz's kitchen is one of the best in Switzerland " !

HOTEL ROSALP
Hotelier: Familie R. Pierroz
Address: CH-1936 Verbier
Phone: (026) 7 63 23   *Telex:* 38322
Dates open: July-Sept & Dec-Apr
No. rooms: 14   *With shower/bath:* 14
Rates: Double room: Sfr 146-256
Credit cards: VS, EC
U.S.Representative: David B. Mitchell
Rep. Telephone No.: (415) 546-1311/SFO
            (212) 696-1323/NYC

 VITZNAU   *PARK HOTEL VITZNAU*

If you want to combine resort style living on the lake and still be within an hour of Lucerne by boat or half an hour by car, then the   Hotel Vitznau might be "your cup of tea." It is ideally located in a beautiful park like setting directly on the banks of Lake Lucerne.

This is not a rustic hotel in any way. Rather, it is sophisticated with all the amenities that one would expect from a deluxe establishment - a large swimming pool, sauna, tennis courts, garden-golf, and even a children's playground. The lakeside setting also allows waterskiing, sailing, swimming, and fishing. The building is like a castle with turrets, towers, gables, and many nooks and crannies. A beautiful lawn surrounded with gardens runs down from the hotel to the edge of the lake to where a promenade follows the contours of the lakefront. The setting is one of such bliss that it is hard to believe you are so close to the city of Lucerne. Inside, the lobby, lounge areas, and dining room are beautifully decorated with combinations of wood beams, fireplaces, oriental rugs on gleaming hardwood floors, green plants, and antique accents.

PARK HOTEL VITZNAU
Hotelier: Peter Bally
Address: CH-6354 Vitznau
Phone: (041) 83 13 22   *Telex:* 78340
Dates open: mid-April to mid-October
No. rooms: 78   *With shower/bath:* 78
Rates: Double room: Sfr 290
U.S.Representative: David B. Mitchell
Rep. Telephone No.: (415) 546-1311/SFO
    (212) 696-1323/NYC

31 WENGEN   *HOTEL REGINA*

It had been many years since I had last visited the Jungfrau area. I remembered it as dramatically beautiful, but I kept getting each of the little towns surrounding the fantastic Jungfrau jumbled in my mind. So when deciding which town to choose to spend the night, I relied upon the advice of my friends Natalie and Craig who always return to their favorite, Wengen.

Wengen is only accessible by train so you need to leave your car at the well marked parking lot at Lauterbrunnen and take the train for the short, beautiful ride up the mountain through heavy forests which open up at regular intervals to give spectacular glimpses of the valley below. When you arrive at Wengen the hotels have porters usually at the station to meet all of the trains. Since there are no cars in Wengen, the porters arrive in cute little motorized carts in which they tuck you and your baggage for the short ride to the hotel. While waiting, I saw one cart brimming with several children, an enormous dog, mother and dad, and all their luggage!

From Wengen train station you can see the Regina Hotel perched on a knoll above the station, only a short walk or ride up a little winding lane. When you enter the hotel you will probably be reminded of one of the British style hotels so popular at the turn of the century. The downstairs has large, rambling lobbies punctuated with small seating areas with chairs surrounding game tables and a huge fireplace surrounded by overstuffed chairs. It all looked very "Swiss British". Our bedroom was quite ordinary *EXCEPT FOR THE VIEW!* And what a view! The "picture" from the balcony, across green fields dropping off to a deep valley below with the valley walls laced with waterfalls and stupendous mountains as a backdrop, was truly one of the most beautiful I have ever seen. The bedroom itself was very undistinquished in decor, but then how could anything within our room compete with the show that nature was providing out our window?

The dining room of the Regina is quite modern and lacking in "country inn" atmosphere. The food was good, but not outstanding... more like plain home cooking. Why then, you might wonder, with simple food and indistinguishable rooms would I include the Regina? The answer is simple. I fell in love with the glory of the view, and I fell in love with the owner, Jack Meyer. He is one of the warmest, most delightful, old-fashioned owners one could possibly imagine. Jack Meyer's family has been in the hotel business for many generations. For him, running a hotel is far more than a business. It is an art and a way of life... a life where the hotel and its operation is a matter of supreme pride.

Content with the hotel, guests return year after year they from all corners of the world. Many of them have met other guests while at the hotel and coincide their holidays with those friends. This is really more like a house party than a hotel and would make a wonderful television serial! Jack Meyer knows all of his guests, remembering their favorite room, their favorite bottle of Scotch, their special pillow. If he sees someone sitting alone, seemingly shy or perhaps lonesome, he finds a way to be sure they are included amongst the other guests. He also has an eye for romance. His wife Erika says some day he will be arrested as a gigolo - "But" says Jack, "If I see a man alone in one corner and a woman alone in another corner, why not invite them both to join me for a cup of coffee? And if I see they enjoy each others' company, what harm is there if I suddenly get called to the office and forget to come back?" This anecdote is so typical of all that is the best of the Swiss Hoteliers. Jack Meyer feels a tremendous responsibility for his guests and is the perfect host.

Jack Meyer's father was in the hotel business, as was his grandfather. I asked Mr. Meyer if he had sons? "Yes" he said with a disappointed look, "I have two, but neither wanted to follow in the profession. However," he added with his delightful smile, "They both changed their minds and are now in hotel school!" How relieved I was that the Meyer family tradition will continue!

HOTEL REGINA
Hotelier: Erika and Jack Meyer
Address: CH-3823 Wengen
Phone: (036) 55 15 12   *Telex:* 923 242
Dates open: June-Sept and Dec-April
No. rooms: 110   *With shower/bath:* 100
Rates: Double room w/bath: Sfr 100-140
Credit cards: AE, VS, DC, EC
U.S.Representative: Swissair

In the small town of Worb, just a few miles east of Berne, is the Hotel Lowen. Charm radiates from its colorful, shuttered exterior and is carried through to its interior. On the entry level the inn has a number of small, delightful dining rooms. If your base is Berne and Worb proves to be just a day excursion, arrange your trip to include a lunch or dinner stop at the Hotel Lowen as it is famous for its superb cuisine. The accommodations are simple, tasteful and attractive in their furnishings. The Hotel Lowen was established over six hundred years ago and has been under the management of the Bernard family for over eleven generations. The service and quality of the inn has been perfected over time and is a marvelous example of one of Switzerland's most highly regarded professions.

HOTEL LOWEN
Hotelier: Familie Hans P. Bernhard
Address: Enggisteinstrasse 3
　　　　　CH-3076 Worb
Phone: (031) 83 23 03
Dates open: All Year
No. rooms: 14 　　*With shower/bath:* 8
Rates: Double room: Sfr 100-130
Credit cards: VS, AE, MC, EC, DC
U.S.Representative: Romantik Hotels
Rep. Telephone No.: (800) 826-0015

The Hotel Julen is found across the bridge on the outskirts of Zermatt with the Matterhorn as a magnificent backdrop. Its relaxing atmosphere is a haven from the hustle and bustle of the heart of town. The Julen, owned and operated by the Julen Family, is definitely a wonderful exception to so many of the new hotels which are clean and attractive but do not offer much "olde worlde" charm. From the moment you enter the lobby and see the cozy fireplace and the comfortable leather sofas, you will feel the mood of relaxation and friendliness. Even more, as you visit the several restaurants you will be captivated by the extremely clever use of antiques, flowers and copper pieces. The hotel is decorated with wonderful taste incorporating comfort with style. The bedrooms are in the simple, clean-lined, light wood furniture so typical of Swiss inns. They are attractive but not decorated with antiques. A few rooms at the rear on the upper floors have the delightful advantage of views of the Matterhorn from their balconies. There is an outdoor terrace behind the hotel for luxuriating in the sun and mountain air. I wish for crisp clear days during your visit to Zermatt, for its natural beauty is the type of experience which makes life long memories.

HOTEL JULEN
Hotelier: Familie Meinrad Julen
Address: CH-3920 Zermatt
Phone: (028) 67 24 81   *Telex:* 472 111
Dates open: All Year
No. rooms: 36   *With shower/bath:* 36
Rates: Double room: Sfr 130
Credit cards: AE, VS, EC
U.S.Representative: Romantik Hotels
Rep. Telephone No.: (800) 826-0015

The richly timbered facade of the Tenne is all that one could possibly hope for in the alpine haven of Zermatt. However, the interior decor somewhat jars the image of a rustic mountain retreat. A rather gaudy, turquoise painted pool dominates the front lawn, and an electronic game machine is placed in the lobby. The bedrooms are very large with modern bathrooms, but again the decor does not appear well coordinated or achieve a feeling of coziness. Some of the rooms have views of Zermatt's pride, the Matterhorn, and yet vistas are marred by the distraction of the facing railroad tracks. With the intention to present to you a list of the most "perfect" of country inns, it was, at first, my decision not to include the Tenne.

Good friends joined us for a portion of our "research" and were with us when we stayed at the Tenne. It was definitely the consensus that the dining experience in the marvelous restaurant at the Tenne Hotel was one of the most memorable of our entire trip in Switzerland - or anywhere else in our travels! Therefore, I found a rebellion resulted when I brought up for discussion the possibility of deleting the Tenne. "After such a meal", they asked, "how could I even consider not including this hotel?" It is true. The food, wine and service excelled. The restaurant is absolutely beautiful. Located in a weathered, old wooden chalet attached to the hotel, the decor blends lovely antiques with exquisite taste and style. We each sampled delicacies from the menu, and each was persistent in proclaiming "theirs" was the most delicious -the best choice.! My veal, smothered in wine and black mushrooms, was so tender it honestly could be cut with a butter knife. Grilled on an open fire, the lamb chops were a gourmet's delight and artistically presented with the freshest of vegetables.

The decorating of the hotel portion of the Tenne is not outstanding in my opinion, but I would like to rave about the management. In a fine hotel there are many touches which are simple, but noticeable. When these little "extras" of detail are added together they leave a total impression of excellence. As an example, at the Tenne the bed linens were freshly ironed and the quality so fine that they felt like silk. After dinner I returned to my room to find the bed covers neatly turned down and my night gown artistically draped across the pillow. In the bathroom the towels were luxuriously large and fluffy.

The principal of the majority cannot be denied! No matter what shortcomings I felt the Tenne might have in terms of its decor, they are vastly overshadowed by the outstanding quality of service and the culinary genius of the kitchen. The Tenne is to be recommended, especially for the discriminating, gourmet traveler!

HOTEL TENNE
Hotelier: Familie J. Stopfer
Address: CH-3920 Zermatt
Phone: (028) 67 18 01   *Telex:* 38170
Dates open: Jun-Sept & Dec-May
No. rooms: 30   *With shower/bath:* 30
Rates: Double room: Sfr 170-225

Your first hint of the elegance of the Seiler Hotel Mont Cervin is noticed as you enter Zermatt and see the magnificent, red, horse drawn carriage proudly waiting at the train station to whisk its privileged guests to the hotel. Although some of the hotels have reverted to simple electric carts to transport guests to their hotels - not the Seiler family! In regal splendor the Seiler's coach awaits with a beautifully uniformed chauffeur. In winter the elegant carriage is converted to a romantic sleigh to quietly glide you to your hotel.

The Seiler Family is an integral part of the very heart of Zermatt. It was back in the mid 1800's when Alexander Seiler ventured into the hotel business with the first hotel in Zermatt - the Monte Rosa. The following generations have continued in the wonderful tradition of hospitality set by him by expanding the family enterprise to include several of the finest hotels in Zermatt. Of these, the Hotel Mont Cervin is the most elegant. As you enter the elaborate front lobby it is hard to believe you could be in a tiny little village. The reception area is decorated with sophisticated charm. The ceilings are high with lovely paneling in some areas, and wooden beams in others. There are flowers everywhere and accents of lovely antiques. The dining room has a tranquil formality combined with a reputation for excellence of gourmet food and exquisite service.

The hotel has many of the modern amenities such as conference rooms, an indoor swimming pool, a sauna, a solarium, and even a kindergarten in the winter for the supervision of children while their parents enjoy the mountain slopes.

While at the Mont Cervin, even if you are not a guest there, stroll into the garden to see the statue of an early mountaineer donated by the Zermatt mountain guides in fond memory of Alexander and Katherina Seiler, the founders of the Seiler hotel chain, and founders of tourism in Zermatt!

SEILER HOTEL MONT CERVIN
Hotelier: Urs H. Keller
Address: CH-3920 Zermatt
Phone: (028) 66 11 21　　*Telex:* 38329
Dates open: 26 Nov-mid October
No. rooms: 129　　*With shower/bath:* 115
Rates: Double room: Sfr 225-360,
　　On a demi-pension basis
Credit cards: AX, DC, VS, MC
U.S.Representative: H.R.I.
Rep. Telephone No.: (800) 223-6800

 ZERMATT　　　　*SEILER HOTEL MONTE ROSA*

The Hotel Monte Rosa is a "must" when discussing the hotels of Zermatt. How could one possibly leave out the original hotel in Zermatt which is so intricately interwoven with the history and romance of this wonderful old village? Not only is the Monte Rosa part of the very essence of Zermatt, but so is the Seiler Family who owns the hotel. It was Alexander Seiler, owner of the Monte Rosa, who waved good-bye to the now famous Englishman, Edward Whymper, on July 13, 1865 as he began his historic climb to become the first man to conquer the Matterhorn. Back in the 1800's Edward Whymper described the fame of the Monte Rosa thus: "If anyone inquired, *What is the best hotel in Zermatt? or Where shall we go?* , the answer was always the same *GO TO THE MONTE ROSA - GO TO SEILER'S*".

The answer really has not changed much over the past century. The small hotel owned by Alexander Seiler has now expanded into a tiny family "kingdom" as each generation of Seilers has inherited the genius of hotel management. There are now several Seiler hotels proudly dominating the hotel scene in Zermatt, but it is still the original Monte Rosa which exudes the nostalgia of the old Zermatt - the romantic Zermatt of yore when adventurous young men sought be be the first to conquer the mountain giants.

SEILER HOTEL MONTE ROSA
Hotelier: Urs H. Keller
Address: CH-3920 Zermatt
Phone: (028) 67 19 22   *Telex:* 38328
Dates open: November to mid-October
No. rooms: 59   *With shower/bath:* 55
Rates: Double room: Sfr 120-175,
      On a demi-pension basis
U.S.Representative: H.R.I.
Rep. Telephone No.: (800) 223-6800

 ZURICH   *HOTEL FLORHOF*

I had heard only glowing reports of both the charm and hospitality provided by the Hotel Florhof, and was therefore very pleased to be able to secure a reservation. A small hotel, more than four hundred years old, the Hotel Florhof is located on the north side of the Limmat River, on a small quiet street that twists up from the little squares and alleys of old Zurich. Removed from the bustle of activity but close enough to walk to all the attractions, the Florhof is more like a residence than a hotel. It is painted a pretty gray blue, and boasts an intimate patio at the rear perfect for summer dining. Just off the lobby is a cozy sitting area with a fireplace and friendly grouping of chairs. The dining room is beautiful and the atmosphere is dominated by a marvelous old blue and white tile stove. Oriental rugs grace the stairways and on each landing is a handsome armoire. The bedrooms are large and bright, with very nice bathrooms. However, they are furnished in rather dated "Danish modern" with a few prints hung haphazardly on the walls. I had hoped for a better balance of warmth and charm, but still found the Florhof to be the best sampling of a small hotel in Zurich.

Management is the Florhof's greatest asset. It is again one of those marvelously run Swiss hotels where the owner is ever present, gracefully tending to the needs of every guest. The Schilters are friendly, outgoing and warm, the perfect hosts. Mr. Shilter supervises the selection and service of food, and Mrs. Shilter is rather like a lovable aunt, who bustles about the house with her eye on every detail. They make a wonderful team and their hotel a home away from home for all their appreciative guests.

HOTEL FLORHOF
Hotelier: Familie H. Schilter
Address: Florhofgasse 4
         CH-8001 Zurich
Phone: (01) 47 44 70
Dates open: All Year
No. rooms: 33   *With shower/bath:* 33
Rates: Double room: Sfr 120-150
Credit cards: AE, DC, VS, EC, MC

 ZURICH   *HOTEL ZUM STORCHEN*

In spite of now wearing all the dressings of a deluxe hotel, there is no question that the Hotel Zum Storchen fits perfectly into the category of an old country inn. The hotel is so perfectly maintained that it is hard to believe the hospitality of the Hotel Zum Storchen has been appreciated for over 620 years! All the modern amenities have been added for the comfort of twentieth century guests, but the hotel retains a combination of charm and efficiency without losing the wealth, style and exquisite taste of early furnishings.

The Hotel Zum Storchen was strategically built at the narrowest section of the Limmat River as it flowed into the Lake Zurich. At this narrow point a bridge was built which became the crossroads of the trade routes to Italy and Germany. Like many of the old inns that revel in tales of history, romance and intrigue, the Hotel Zum Storchen is no exception. Famous people including Swedish kings, princes, and artists of all kinds have been guests here. There are stories of murder to haunt its past; one of the owner's of the hotel, Katarina von Steg von Uri and her son, accused of murdering an uncle over an inheritance in 1371, were banished from Zurich. My favorite story was that of of a rival hotel owner, Hanns Hennssler, owner of a competitive hotel, the Sword Inn, who brought suit against the owner of the Hotel Zum Storchen in 1477 for stealing guests off the streets and enticing them away from his hotel !

What a change has taken place over the many centuries! No enticing is needed. Now you are very lucky if the Hotel Zum Storchen can find a room for you!

HOTEL ZUM STORCHEN
Hotelier: J. Philippe Jaussi
Address: Am Weinplatz 2
  CH-8001 Zurich
Phone: (01) 211 55 10   *Telex:* 813 354
Dates open: All Year
*No. rooms:*77   *With shower/bath:* 77
Rates: Double room: Sfr 200-280
Credit cards: AX, DC, EC, VS
U.S.Representative: Tourex, NYC

Supplemental Hotel Descriptions

 50 CHIASSO   *HOTEL CORSO*

Alfred J. Haring, CH-6830 Chiasso, Tel: (091) 44 57 01

If you love homemade pasta, maneuver a stopover at the Hotel Corso located in Chiasso on the Italian border. They have the reputation for absolutely superb ravioli!

 39 FEUTERSOEY   *HOTEL ROSSLI*

CH-3784 Feutersoey, Tel (030) 51 012

For local color the Rossli is a real "gem". Located near Gstaad, it is made of wood and filled with Bernese style antique wooden furniture. From the atmospheric dining room with wooden country-style tables and chairs you can look directly into the kitchen. This is where the local farmers come in the afternoon to have a drink of FENDANT (the wonderful, airy, light white local wine) and perhaps their evening meal in the cozy informal restaurant.

 22 KILCHBERG   *OBER MONCHHOF*

CH-8802 Kilchberg

This hotel is so attractive that it is a favorite of my Swiss friend, Jacqueline, when she has foreign visitors. The hotel is located overlooking Lake Zurich just a short drive from the city. The exterior of the hotel is wood and timber while inside the dining rooms have extensive paneling and antique furnishings. It is the restaurant which is famous, but there are also a few rooms for those wanting to spend the night.

 KUSNACHT *HOTEL HERMITAGE*

CH-8700 Kusnacht, Tel: (01) 910 52 22

The Hotel Hermitage is a little oasis near the city of Zurich. The hotel is located in a beautiful parklike setting directly on the shores of Lake Zurich. The food is delicious and the bedrooms delightfully furnished in charming small prints - the "Laura Ashley" look. Many of the bedrooms have balconies where breakfast can be enjoyed in the summertime.

 LENK *HOSTELLERIE KREUZ*

Familie Tritten, CH-3775 Lenk, Tel: (030) 3l3 87

The Hostelerie Kreuz is located in the Simmental Valley in the town of Lenk, a resort offering a top selection of facilities for the tourist including skiing, walking trails, ice skating, fishing, swimming, and tennis.

There are also many excellent hotels to accommodate the tourist, such as the Hostellerie Kreuz dating back to l834. Since that time there have been many renovations - even the addition of an indoor pool. However the Walter Tritten family keep up wonderful traditions such as candle light meals and once weekly special "farm buffet" dinners.

A kind note from Mr. Tritten included a little more information of the restaurant at the Hostellerie Kreuz..."The Kreuz still remains the cozy traditional restaurant it always was. It's the place everybody feels at home. At ease. It's the place where the local farmers meet to talk about their cattle and where they play the local card game, "Jass".

 **MAIENFELD** *SCHLOSS BRANDES*

CH-7304 Maienfeld, Tel: (085) 9 24 23

Schloss Brandes, as the name implies, is a castle hotel, crowning the top of a small stone mound from which it surveys the surrounding vineyards. As you drive up the road to the castle you need to park your car and walk the last short distance before entering through a huge fortess-like portal. The dining room is dramatic with a soaring ceiling. This hotel has tremendous appeal for all castle lovers who like to step back into history. There are many antiques used throughout including some enormous chandeliers. Some of the bedrooms have their own fireplaces. This is a "must" on our next trip to Switzerland!

 RAPPERSWIL *HOTEL HIRSCHEN*

CH-8640 Rapperswil, Tel: (055) 27 66 24

The Hirschen is located in the medieval town of Rapperswil on Lake Zurich. The Hotel Hirschen has only a few rooms but excellent dining and a superb view with extremely kind and cordial hosts.

 SAMEDAN *HOTEL DONATZ*

Family Donatz, CH-7503 Samedan, Tel: (082) 6 46 66

Only a few miles north of St. Moritz is the town of Samedan - a favorite hiking center. You can use Samedan as your base and each day take a train to a nearby town to explore a different network of beautiful walking paths.

In Samedan the Hotel Donatz is a family run hotel - nothing fancy, just genuine hospitality and good cooking. Because the Donatz family is so very involved in the management of this hotel, it becomes quite special. Mr. Donatz is the owner and the capable chef. His mother is still very involved overseeing each detail to ensure the guests are happy. Mr. Donatz's wife is a gracious hostess.

 URSENBACH *LANDGASTHOF HIRSERNBAD*

CH-4937 Ursenbach, tel: (063) 56 32 56

The Landgasthof Hirsernbad is an extremely attractive stucco and wood timbered building with buff colored facade, green shutters, flower boxes filled with geraniums, and wooden tables and chairs set in the rear garden for summer dining. The bedrooms are not outstanding, but the cozy dining room is famous for serving excellent meals.

 VADUZ, LIECHTENSTEIN *HOTEL REAL*

Stadtle 2l, Vaduz, Liechtenstein, Tel: (075) 2 22 22

The Hotel Real is located in in Liechtenstein in the center of the town of Vaduz. The hotel is not imposing in any way. The furniture is nondescript. The decor is just "so so". But the food is incredible - perhaps the best in the whole region - and served exquisitely! Dining here is an experience. The specialties include a wonderful entree called "Prince Constantin" which is a gourmet delight loaded with the local mushrooms. Wild game is also featured on the menu. The dining service is spectacular with crisp white table cloths, silverware, and pretty china.

 **VEVEY** *HOTEL DU LAC*

CH-1800 Vevey, Tel: (021) 51 10 41

The history of the Du Lac is intertwined with that of the hotel community of Lake Geneva. Indeed it was one of the first hotels built on the Riviera Vaudoise -the actual date 1868. Since the hotel opened its doors, it has hosted many of the world's celebrities including the famous author, Henryk Sienkiewiez, author of "Quo Vadis, who resided here from 1914 to 1916. The public rooms of the Du Lac are rather formal with high ceilings and sedate furniture. You can almost visualize gossiping ladies in long skirts disembarking from fancy horse drawn carriages to enter the lobby. Upstairs many of the rooms have lovely views of Lake Geneva.

 ZAZIWIL *GASTHOF APPENBERG*

Familie Mosimann, CH-3532 Zaziwil, Tel: (031) 99 27 21

The Gasthof Appenberg, located in the Emmental Valley, has been highly recommended. The brochure shows a "Picture Book Perfect" Swiss chalet peaking out from beneath a cozy overhanging wooden roof, happy red geraniums snuggled on every balcony, shutters at the windows, and a charming little garden. If the inn itself is only half as marvelous as the photograph, this is a real winner!

The inn on the cover of the brochure is actually one of a series of little chalets owned by the Mosimann family. With imagination and taste they have renovated each into little guest rooms.

Index

Alphabetical Listing of Hotels By Hotel Name

Notes

"INN DISCOVERIES FROM OUR READERS"

Future editions of KAREN BROWN'S COUNTRY INN SERIES are going to include a new feature - a list of hotels recommended by our readers. We have received many letters describing wonderful inns you have discovered; however, we have never included them until we had the opportunity to make a personal inspection. This seemed a waste of some marvelous "tips". So we have started a file to be used in each forthcoming edition of our guide books which will be called "INN DISCOVERIES FROM OUR READERS".

If you have a favorite discovery you would be willing to share with other travellers who love to travel the "inn way" please let us hear from you and include the following information.

1. Your name, address and telephone number

2. Name, address, and telephone of "Your Inn"

3. Brochure or picture of inn (we cannot return photographs)

4. Written permission to use an edited version of your description

5. Would you want your name, city and state included in the book?

In addition to our current guide books which include hotels in France, England, Scotland, Wales, Switzerland, and Italy, we are now researching guide books for all of Europe and would appreciate comments on any of your favorites. The type of inn we would love to hear about are those with special "Olde Worlde" ambiance, charm, and atmosphere. We need a brochure or picture so that we can select those which most closely follow the mood of our guides. We look forward to hearing from you. Thank you very much!

Notes

ORDER FORM

If you have enjoyed this travel guide and would like to receive an additional copy or purchase other books in Karen Brown's travel series on country inns, the following books can be purchased in most major bookstores or ordered directly from the the publisher. These delightful volumes are all similar in style and format and include detailed countryside itineraries and a selective list of charming, atmospheric inns. Lavishly illustrated with original drawings and maps these guides enhance any travel library and make wonderful gifts.

....

PLEASE MAIL TO:

Name: _____ Street _____

City: _____ State _____ Zip _____

I AM ENCLOSING A CHECK TO COVER ($9.95 per copy plus $1.00 per copy postage and handling. California residents please include 6.5% tax)

_____ copies of FRENCH COUNTRY INNS & CHATEAU HOTELS

_____ copies of ENGLISH, WELSH & SCOTTISH COUNTRY INNS

_____ copies of SWISS COUNTRY INNS & CHALETS

_____ copies of ITALIAN COUNTRY INNS & VILLAS

_____ GIFT PACK, all four books at $30.00 plus postage

_____ Please send information on titles to be released

make checks out to:
TRAVEL PRESS
P.O. Box 1477
San Mateo, Ca. 94401

Notes

Footloose

Following the tradition and flavor of other Travel Press publications *FOOTLOOSE* will tempt the countryside traveler to explore unique and interesting destinations. Published quarterly, each issue will whisk you off to some exciting corner of the world; highlight a newly discovered country inn; recommend an international restaurant and share some of their specialties; update gourmet and wine releases; keep you posted on some of the best travel bargains, tours and news items; review the current theater in London, Paris, New York and provide a calendar spotlighting international cultural events.

If you would like to subscribe or receive further information concerning *FOOTLOOSE*, please fill out and mail the form below.

....

———— I AM INTERESTED IN RECEIVING FURTHER INFORMATION ABOUT *FOOTLOOSE*.

Name: ————————————————————

Address: ——————————————————————

City: ———————————— *State:* ——— *Zip:* —————————

Notes

This guide is especially written for the individual traveller. However, should you be interested in having all the details of your holiday preplanned, Town and Country Travel Service designs tours to Europe for small groups using hotels with special charm and appeal. For further information on the Country Inn Holidays we offer, or for custom tours we can plan for your own group or club please call:

TOWN & COUNTRY TRAVEL SERVICE
16 East Third Avenue
San Mateo, CA. 94401

Within California 800 227-6734
Outside California 800 227-6733

KAREN BROWN has spent most of her life in the San Francisco Bay area where she now lives with her devoted German Shepherd, "Andy", in a cozy cottage surrounded by her collection of antiques. When nineteen Karen traveled to Europe where she wrote *French Country Inns and Chateau Hotels* - the first book in what has grown to be an extremely successful series on charming small European hotels. When not writing, Karen has worked as a travel consultant and as a tour guide to Europe. She loves skiing, hiking, cooking, and entertaining. Another hobby is languages. Karen speaks fluent French and German. Her real love though is exploring the world and although she has traveled extensively, staying in a wide variety of accommodations ranging from tents in the Himalayas to safari camps in Africa, her favorite abode is still the small country inn of Europe which she captures so delightfully in her books.